Testing in Scrum

About the Author

Tilo Linz is co-founder and managing director of imbus AG, a leading provider of software testing and quality assurance solutions for more than 20 years. Linz is co-founder of the German Testing Board and a founding member of the ISTQB, where he has contributed widely to the national and international promotion of education and training in this field. He is co-author of *Software Testing Foundations* (also published by Rocky Nook and now in its 4th edition) – one of the most successful and widely-read books on the subject.

Every day, Linz is faced with the many opportunities and challenges presented by the introduction of agile development methods, whether in the course of customer projects or the continuing development of imbus' own Test*Bench* product and the introduction of Kanban methodology as a basis for the company's marketing strategy.

Tilo Linz

Testing in Scrum

A Guide for Software Quality Assurance
in the Agile World

Tilo Linz (www.softwaretest-knowledge.net, www.imbus.de)

Editor: Michael Barabas
Copyeditor: Judy Flynn
Translator: Jeremy Cloot
Layout: Josef Hegele
Project Manager: Matthias Rossmanith
Cover Design: Helmut Kraus, www.exclam.de

ISBN 978-1-937538-39-2

1st Edition 2014
© 2014 by Tilo Linz

Rocky Nook Inc.
802 East Cota St., 3rd Floor
Santa Barbara, CA 93103

www.rockynook.com

Copyright © 2013 by dpunkt.verlag GmbH, Heidelberg, Germany.
Title of the German original: Testen in Scrum-Projekten
ISBN: 978-3-89864-799-1
Translation Copyright © 2014 by Rocky Nook. All rights reserved.

Linz, Tilo.
  Testing in Scrum : a guide for software quality assurance in the agile world / Tilo Linz. -- 1st edition.
     pages cm
  ISBN 978-1-937538-39-2 (paperback)
  1. Scrum (Computer software development) 2. Agile software development. 3. Computer software--Testing.
  4. Computer software--Quality control. I. Title.
  QA76.76.D47L548 2014
  005.1'4--dc23
                              2014000961

Distributed by O'Reilly Media
1005 Gravenstein Highway North
Sebastopol, CA 95472

Acknowledgments

Even if it is my name that appears on the cover, this book wouldn't have been possible without the advice and support of many of my colleagues.

I would particularly like to thank the interviewees and authors of the case studies, who also acted as reviewers and sounding boards: Dr. Stephan Albrecht at Avid, Dierk Engelhardt at imbus, Andrea Heck at Siemens, Eric Hentschel at ImmobilienScout24, Sabine Herrmann at zooplus, Joachim Hofer at imbus and Terry Zuo at GE Oil & Gas. The many interesting conversations we had provided plenty of valuable insights into the implementation of agile development techniques and the real-world use of Scrum.

I would also like to thank my expert reviewers for their valuable comments, suggestions, and corrections: Oliver Gradl at Siemens for his input on agile integration and system testing, Dr. Stefan Kriebel at BMW and Horst Pohlmann for their feedback on embedded systems, Stefan Schmitz at iq-stz for his profound knowledge of the ISO 9000 standard and auditing, Uwe Vigenschow at oose Innovative Informatik for the fruitful discussions on the subject of acceptance testing and Prof. Mario Winter at the University of Cologne who, in spite of being involved in a book project of his own, contributed his time as a reviewer and offered important input for the chapter on integration testing. Thanks also go to all the other reviewers whose names are not mentioned here.

Thanks, too, go to the entire staff at imbus for their valuable advice and time spent supporting this project, especially Arne Becher, Dr. Christian Brandes, Thomas Roßner and Carola Wittigschlager. My heartfelt thanks also go to Claudia Wissner, without whom many of the illustrations would not have progressed beyond the sketch stage.

Thanks also go out to Matthias Rossmanith at Rocky Nook for his tireless help during the production of this book and his patience when an extra sprint or two were required.

And, last but not least, a big thank you to my wife, Sabine, and our daughters, Lisa and Lena, who had to survive without me for many long evenings and weekends while I worked on the text.

I wish you an interesting read and every success applying these techniques in your own testing environment.

Tilo Linz, February 2014

Contents

1 Introduction

Software is everywhere. Virtually every complex product manufactured today is controlled by software, and many commercial services are based on software systems. The quality of the software used is therefore a crucial factor when it comes to remaining competitive. The faster a company can integrate new software in its products or bring software products to market, the greater the opportunity to beat the competition.

Agile software development methods are designed to reduce time to market (TTM) and improve software quality while increasing the relevance of products to customer needs. It is no surprise that the use of agile methodology is on the increase in large international projects as well as in product development at all manner of large corporations. In most cases, this means switching from the tried and trusted V model to agile testing using Scrum methodology.

However, switching to agile and learning to use it effectively and productively is not always easy, especially when multiple teams are involved. Every team member, project manager and all members of line management have to make significant changes to the way they work. Particularly, the effectiveness of software testing and quality assurance (QA) are crucial to the success of introducing and using agile methodology in a team, a department or an entire company, and will determine whether its potential advantages can be put into practice.

Most literature on the subject of agile methodology (including many of the works referenced in the bibliography at the end of this book) is written from the viewpoint of software developers and programmers, and tends to place its main emphasis on programming techniques and agile project management—testing is usually only mentioned in the guise of unit testing and its associated tools. In other words, it concentrates on testing from the developer's point of view. However, unit tests alone are not sufficient and broader-based testing is crucial to the success of agile development processes.

The aim of this book is to close this gap and describe the agile development process from the viewpoint of testing and QA. It shows how agile testing works and details where traditional testing techniques are still necessary within the agile environment and how to embed these in the agile approach.

1.1 Target Audience

Understanding how testing in agile projects works

On one hand, this book is aimed at beginners who are just starting to work with agile methodology, who are due to work in agile projects or who are planning to introduce (or have already introduced) Scrum into a project or team.

- We provide tips and advice on how product development managers, project managers, test managers, and QA managers can help to realize the full potential of agile methodology.
- Professional (certified) testers and software quality experts will learn how to work effectively in agile teams and make optimal use of their expertise. You will also learn how to adapt your working style to fit into the agile environment.

Augmenting your knowledge of (automated) testing and agile quality assurance techniques

On the other hand, we are also aiming at readers who already have experience working in agile teams and wish to expand their knowledge of testing and QA techniques to increase productivity and product quality.

- Product Owners, Scrum Masters, QA operatives, and members of management teams will learn how systematic, highly automated testing works and about the importance of providing continual, reliable and comprehensive feedback on the quality of the software being developed.
- Programmers, testers, and other agile team members will learn how to apply highly automated testing methods to unit, integration and system tests.

The text includes a wealth of practical examples and practice questions, making it well suited as a textbook or for self-teaching.

1.2   Book Contents

Chapter 2 provides a brief overview of the currently popular Scrum and Kanban methodologies and an overview of the most important agile management methods for managers looking to implement agile methods in their departments. These methods are compared with traditional methods to give you an idea of the changes that introducing agile methods involves. Readers who are already familiar with Scrum and Kanban methodology can skip this chapter.

Chapter 2

Chapter 3 details the lightweight planning and control tools that Scrum uses in place of traditional project planning tools. Remember, working in an agile fashion doesn't mean working aimlessly! Chapter 3, too, is aimed primarily at readers who are making the switch to agile development. Nevertheless, the explanations and tips regarding the importance of planning tools for constructive quality assurance and error prevention will be useful to experienced readers too.

Chapter 3

Chapter 4 covers unit testing and "test first" programming techniques. Topics include what unit tests can be expected to achieve and how they can be automated. This chapter covers the basics of unit testing techniques and tools and will help system testers, test specialists, and project team members with little or no unit testing experience to work more closely and effectively with programmers and unit testers. It also includes a wealth of useful tips that will help experienced programmers and testers to improve their testing techniques. We also explain the test first test-driven approach to programming and its importance within agile projects.

Chapter 4

Chapter 5 covers integration testing and the concept of continuous integration testing. Integration testing covers test cases that even the most diligent programmers miss when using unit tests. This chapter covers all the basics of software integration and integration testing, and introduces continuous integration techniques, explaining how to use them within a project.

Chapter 5

Chapter 6 discusses system testing and the concept of nonstop testing. Based on system testing foundations, this chapter explains how to use agile techniques to perform manual tests. It also explains how to automate system tests and embed them in the continuous integration process. This chapter is aimed not only at system testers and other testing specialists, but also at programmers who wish to better understand agile testing techniques that lie outside their usual development-driven remit.

Chapter 6

Chapter 7   Chapter 7 compares traditional and agile ideas of quality assurance and explains the constructive and preventative QA practices that are built in to Scrum. This chapter includes tips on how to perform agile QA and explains how all QA specialists can use their know-how within agile projects and contribute to the success of agile projects.

Chapter 8   Chapter 8 presents six industrial, e-commerce, and software development case studies. These reflect the experiences gained and lessons learned by the interviewees during the introduction and application of agile techniques.

Chapter Overview   Chapters 2, 3, 7, and 8 discuss process and management topics and are aimed at readers who are more interested in the management aspect of the subject. Chapters 4, 5, and 6 discuss (automated) agile testing at various levels and are oriented toward more technically minded readers. Because agile testing is not the same as unit, we also explain in detail the aims of and differences between unit, integration, and system testing.

Figure 1-1 provides a visual overview of the book's structure:

Fig. 1–1
The structure of the book

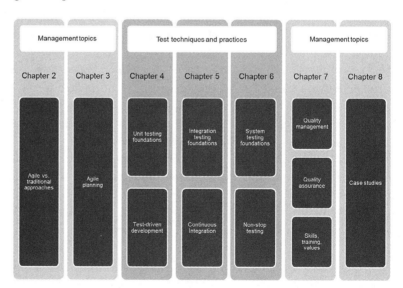

Case study, checks   According to most popular literature on the subject, many agile concepts,
and exercises   techniques and practices are simple to implement. Similarly, the ideas, advice and tips covered in the following chapters may at first appear simple, but the sticking points often only become evident in the course of implementation. To help you understand and experience the challenges involved, the text includes:

- A fictional case study that illustrates the methodology and techniques being discussed.
- Checks and exercises to help you recap the content discussed in each chapter and scrutinize your own situation and behavior within your project.

1.3   Case Study

The fictional case study the book refers to uses the following scenario. The company eHome Tools is a developer of home automation systems based on the following elements:

- **Actuators:**
Lamps and other electrical devices are connected by means of electronic switches. Every actuator is connected by wire or wirelessly to a comms bus that can be used to control it remotely.

- **Sensors:**
Thermal, wind and humidity detectors and simple contact sensors (for example, to indicate an open window) can also be connected to the bus.

- **Bus:**
Switching instructions and status signals for the actuators and sensors are sent via the bus to the central controller in the form of "telegrams."

- **Controller:**
The central controller sends switching signals to the actuators (e.g., "switch kitchen light on") and receives status signals from the sensors (e.g., "kitchen temperature 20 degrees") and actuators (e.g., "kitchen light is on"). The controller is either event-driven (i.e., reacts to incoming signals) or works on the basis of timed commands (e.g., "8pm → close kitchen blind").

- **User interface:**
The controller has a user interface that visualizes the current status of all elements of the eHome and enables its inhabitants to send instructions (e.g., "switch kitchen light off") via mouse click to the house systems.

Case Study: eHome Controller

eHome Tools has many competitors and, in order to remain competitive, the company decides to develop new controller software. An increasing number of customers is asking for software that can be controlled via smartphones and other mobile devices, so it is clear from the start that this project has to be completed quickly if it is to be successful. It is essential that the new system is extensible and open for third-party devices. If the new system is able to control devices from other manufacturers, management is convinced that the company can win over customers who wish to extend their existing systems. To fulfill this goal, the new system has to support as wide a range of existing third-party hardware as possible and must be capable of adapting to support new devices as soon as they appear on the market.

In view of these challenges, the decision is taken to develop the new system using agile methodology and to release an updated version of the controller software (with support for new devices and protocols) every month.

1.4　Website

The code samples included in the text are available for download at the book's website [URL: SWT-knowledge]. Feel free to use them to construct your own test cases.

The practice questions and exercises are also available online and can be commented on. We look forward to discussing your comments and suggestions.

In spite of all our efforts and those of the publisher, it is still possible that some text errors remain. Any necessary corrections will be published online.

2   Agile vs. Traditional Approaches

This chapter provides overviews of the Scrum agile project management framework and the popular Kanban project management methodology. Kanban was developed from lean production theory and shows some similarities to Scrum. We will compare both methodologies with traditional process models. If you are involved in managing a project or department-wide switch to agile working methods, this chapter will give you an overview of the organizational changes that are necessary on company, department and project team levels. If you are already familiar with the workings of Scrum and/or Kanban, you can skip this chapter.

2.1   Scrum

Scrum is an agile[1] project management framework first introduced in 1999 by Ken Schwaber in his article *Scrum: A Pattern Language for Hyperproductive Software Development* [Beedle et al. 99]. The 2002 book *Agile Software Development with Scrum* [Schwaber/Beedle 02] helped Scrum methodology to reach a wider audience.

Scrum does not determine which specific techniques software developers should use (refactoring, for example) and instead leaves such decisions to the development team itself. This usually leads to the use of Extreme Programming[2] (XP) techniques, which are then introduced in

---

1.   The term "agile" is used to describe lightweight software development processes that are very different from traditional heavyweight methods. The term was coined at a developer conference in Utah in 2001, where the *Agile Manifest* was first drafted (see [URL: Agile Manifesto]).

2.   Extreme Programming (XP) is a loose collection of values, principles and practices for agile software development introduced by Kent Beck in 1999. Most agile development processes are based on the tenets of XP. The current version of XP is explained by Beck in [Beck/Andres 04].

the course of the switch to Scrum. Additionally, Scrum does not dictate the types of tests that an agile project is subjected to.

Agile practices for management

The Scrum framework describes a set of practices for managing (software) projects that radically alters the processes involved and replaces the traditional deterministic planning approach with an adaptive, empirical project control system [Schwaber/Beedle 02]. The main aim of using Scrum is to enable a project team to react quickly, simply and appropriately instead of wasting time and energy creating, implementing and updating outdated plans.

The basic project management instruments used by Scrum are:

▪ **Sprint:**
Scrum divides a project into short, fixed-length iterations called Sprints[3]. The idea here is that a Sprint that lasts just three or four weeks can be planned and managed more simply and effectively than release cycles that are as long as a year or more (see [Schwaber/Beedle 02, p. 52]).

▪ **Product Increment:**
The product grows with each iteration so each Sprint results in a working and potentially releasable/shippable product (called an increment).

▪ **Product Backlog:**
If planning is reduced to a one-dimensional list of goals, a project becomes much less complex, and this is exactly what Scrum is all about. The Product Owner (see below) keeps a record called the Product Backlog, which, according to [Pichler 10], contains all known requirements and results that have to be implemented or achieved to complete the project successfully. These include functional and non-functional requirements as well as interface specifications. The Product Backlog can also include work items such as the structure of the test and development environment and debugging. The product requirement entries in the list are prioritized in relation to one another, but no further interdependencies or timing stipulations are included. The Product Backlog is not set in stone and changes constantly with the completion of each Sprint. Keeping the Backlog up to date is known as Backlog Refinement or Backlog Grooming. The Product Owner is

---

3.   The "sprint" metaphor refers not to high speed, but to the short courses involved in sprint racing.

responsible for adding new requirements and, if necessary, breaking them down into smaller units as soon as the entire team has understood the new requirement. Requirements are subject to constant analysis and reprioritizing. Obsolete requirements are deleted. Put succinctly, Scrum makes planning simpler and more reliable because all factors that makes conventional planning unreliable are avoided.

Sprint Backlog:

Of course, in reality things aren't quite that simple. A complex software development project cannot be managed using just a long list of prioritized requirements, and a Scrum Team has to decide which team members have to perform which tasks and when. The team members and the Product Owner make these decisions step by step for each Sprint in turn. At the start of a Sprint, the team takes the prioritized tasks at the top of the Product Backlog list and uses them to create a more concise Sprint Backlog. At this point, it is essential that the requirements in the new Backlog have been properly understood and precisely worded. Requirements that do not fulfill these criteria (the "Definition of Ready") are not yet ready to be included in the Sprint. This is the point at which decisions regarding the interdependencies between the requirements, the resulting tasks, the effort involved and the timing of the entire Sprint are made. All the tasks that the team deems necessary to the success of the pending Sprint are now entered in the Sprint Backlog.

Definition of Done:

To ensure that the Sprint results in a working product increment (a potentially shippable product), the team drafts criteria that enable it to assess whether the work on the increment is complete [URL: Scrum Guide]. The criteria used are described as the team's "Definition of Done" (DoD) and can be drafted as a global checklist for the entire Sprint or with relation to individual tasks within it. Discussion of the appropriateness of ready criteria is crucial to the clear definition of requirements and tasks within the team, although these only ever apply to the current Sprint. The planning horizon is short-term and the scope of work to be done is small in comparison with the overall project. This approach means the team is clearly focused and that the Sprint Backlog cannot be altered during the current Sprint (see [Pichler 10]). This type of plan has a good chance of being completed successfully.

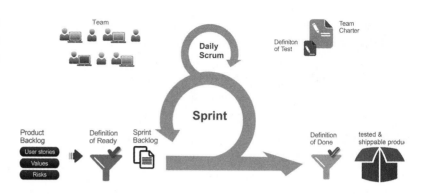

Fig. 2–1
The basic principles of the
Scrum process

▨ **Timeboxing:**

Every Sprint is required to deliver a potentially shippable product[4]. In turn, this means that the Sprint Backlog should only contain tasks that contribute to the shippability of the resulting product. Any components of the product that cannot be completed during the Sprint have to be left out and, to avoid this happening, the team needs to select the features that can be realistically completed at the start of the Sprint. In case of doubt, shippable always takes priority over functionality—a principle known as "timeboxing." If timeboxing is to be successful, the team has to estimate the amount of work involved in completing all the features that it wishes to include in the Sprint. Features that require too much work are left out, divided into smaller tasks or have the scope of their targeted functionality reduced. As with traditional planning processes, Scrum Teams have to engage in effort estimation, although two important factors ensure that Scrum-based estimations are more accurate than traditional ones:

- The team only has to consider the work involved in the pending Sprint. The tasks involved are of a manageable size and, thanks to previously completed Sprints, the team is usually well prepared.
- Estimations are made by means of Planning Poker—another XP technique (see section 3.5). The estimations made by individual team members can vary a lot, but are pretty accurate on average.

Timeboxing takes place not only in Sprints but also in other situations that require the team to be done. For example, it can be used to ensure that meetings begin punctually and only run for the allotted time.

---

4. "Incremental deliveries of 'done' product ensure that a potentially useful version of the working product is always available" [URL: Scrum Guide].

Transparency:

Transparency is one of the most powerful Scrum tools. The Sprint Backlog is maintained publicly on a whiteboard[5], which makes the content and progress of the current Sprint easily comprehensible for the team, management and any other interested parties. The board contains requirements and their associated tasks, arranged in rows, while the columns represent the current state of each task (to do, in progress, or completed). The Sprint Status is updated daily during the Daily Scrum, and the individual task cards are shifted across the board according to the current progress of each task. Figure 2-2 shows the Test*Bench* team's whiteboard (see case study 8.2). The transparency provided by updating the whiteboard during the Daily Scrum means that every team member knows what is going on around them (which helps to prevent team members working at cross purposes) and everyone is aware of the progress of everyone else's tasks, which automatically induces pressure to succeed within the team. The team is compelled to discuss and solve problems that occur[6]. Once difficulties are

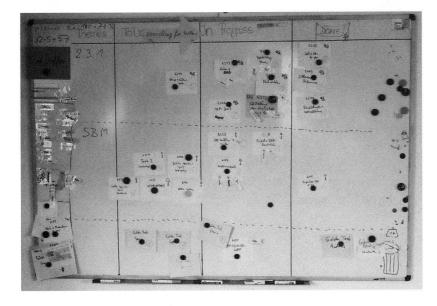

Fig. 2–2

*The Test*Bench *team's whiteboard*

---

5. A mobile partition wall makes a good alternative. If your team uses IT-based tools, the Sprint Backlog should be displayed in a prominent position on a large monitor in the team room.
6. They cannot be hidden anyway.

in the open, it is much easier to offer or accept help. Additionally, daily discussions of tasks and results provides a steady stream of success stories for each team member and the team as a whole.

Allocating roles within the team   Alongside these project management techniques, the importance of the team and role allocation are also defined differently in a Scrum environment. The Scrum model stipulates just three major roles within the team (after [Schwaber/Beedle 02, ch. 3]):

- The **Scrum Master** is a new type of management role. It is the person responsible for ensuring that Scrum practices are implemented and carried out. If these practices should become overstretched or impeded in any way, it is the Scrum Master's job to halt the process or find an alternative solution. A Scrum Master has no real authority, but instead acts as a coach. Process-related impediments can often be solved by explaining the process to the team, reminding it of the appropriate procedures or by running a dedicated workshop. Other impediments (for example, a non-functioning build environment) sometimes require additional resources (such as a faster build server or a more appropriate tool) and it may be necessary to allocate better-qualified team members to the build process. A Scrum Master should never delegate an unsolved issue back to the team. If this happens regularly, the solution is usually to find a new Scrum Master.

- The **Product Owner** is responsible for keeping the Product Backlog up to date, and represents the interface between the customer and the team[7]. The Product Owner decides which features are to be implemented—in other words he/she is responsible for determining the nature of the product. In practice, the Product Owner role can be filled by the current product manager, a team leader or the project head[8]. The Product Owner has no authority as team leader and does not oversee the overall Scrum process, which is the responsibility of the Scrum Master.

---

7.   If the project at hand involves customer-specific specifications, the Product Owner can be a member of the customer's own team.
8.   People from different backgrounds approach the Product Owner role in different ways and will run the Product Backlog according to their own skills and preferences. All team members should be aware of this, especially when Scrum is first implemented.

The **Development Team**[9] usually comprises between three and nine members who fulfill all the tasks necessary to complete the product, Sprint for Sprint. "A Scrum (development) team should include people with all the skills necessary to meet the Sprint Goal. Scrum eschews vertical teams of analysts, designers, quality control, and coding engineers. A Scrum (development) team self-organizes so that everyone contributes to the outcome. Each team member applies his or her expertise to all of the problems. The resultant synergy from a tester helping a designer construct code improves code quality and increases productivity. Regardless of the team composition, it is responsible for doing all the analysis, design, coding, testing, and user documentation" ([Schwaber/ Beedle 02]).

Accordingly, teams should be cross-functional[10]. This is difficult to achieve and usually means that, rather than building a team in which everyone has comparable skills, all team members are willing to work on all the current tasks using their own particular skills. Scrum is all about optimizing the abilities and performance of the team as a whole.

The fact that Scrum advocates the use of cross-functional teams and flat hierarchies within the team is often misunderstood. Cross-functional means that team members work on a multi-functional basis. For example, a system architect and a programmer create an architecture together and the architect helps the programmer during the coding phase, perhaps learning along the way that theoretical system designs can be quite difficult to implement. By the same token, a tester can help a programmer to define the right unit tests, perhaps learning how to automate testing in the process. Nevertheless, every team member has his or her own specific skills and uses these to lead current events. The point is that no-one is in a position to make statements such as, "I'm a tester and I don't do anything else." Case studies 8.1 and 8.4 particularly illustrate some of the stumbling blocks that you might encounter during the switch to Scrum methodology.

Multi-functional teams

---

9. "A Scrum Team comprises a Product Owner, the development team and the Scrum Master." [URL: Scrum Guide]. [Schwaber/Beedle 02] does not yet fully differentiate between team and development team, which is why the term is used in brackets above.
10. In XP [Beck/Andres 04] this concept is known as the One Team Principle, whereas Scrum [Schwaber/Beedle 02] calls it a cross-functional team.

Case Study 2–1

> **The eHome Controller Project 2-1: Project Setup**
>
> The decision to implement the project includes a budget that covers three developers, one tester, a Product Owner and a part-time Scrum Master.
>
> The ideas about who should belong to the team are varied. Some voices advocate the best personnel, others argue for the most experienced, while still others would prefer to see new staff members with new ideas. The members of the existing team also have varying views on the introduction of Scrum. While some think it is long overdue, others are of the opinion that you cannot teach an old dog new tricks. Some think that they already work in an agile fashion, while the more technically-minded members of the team are concerned that it will be impossible to guarantee nonstop functionality of precisely defined bus protocols and predefined standards without the use of traditional specifications and documentation.
>
> In the end, the necessity of filling the roles within the team with appropriate know-how made the decisions relatively simple. At least one of the developers has to know all about the bus protocols and device hardware (for the company's own products as well as those of the competition), and this know-how is already available in-house. A creative Web developer should be in charge of the user interface, so this position requires fresh recruitment. The current head of the software team takes on the role of Product Owner.
>
> Because the team has no prior experience of Scrum methodology, an independent consultant is hired as Scrum Master and is responsible for teaching the team all about Scrum techniques and practices as well as communicating with management and ensuring that the team doesn't fall back into its old ways.
>
> The project is given the go-ahead for a 12 month period and the marketing team has requested that the trial period includes four product releases. In other words, the first release has to be ready in three months!

Feature teams   Large, complex projects have to be divided up between multiple Scrum Teams. Some projects are divided up along system architecture lines, resulting in component-oriented teams, while others use feature teams that work on groups of requirements in multiple Sprints covering various system components—an approach known as global code ownership. Case study 8.5, "Scrum in a Medical Technology Environment," is an example of this approach.

In theory, the advantage of this approach is that a feature team works on all the current requirements and therefore has a more customer-centric view of the project. The downside of this approach is that a feature team has (again, theoretically) less in-depth knowledge of the individual software components, leading to slower and more error-prone design, coding and testing. Every project team has to decide for itself which model works best under the given circumstances.

2.2 Kanban

Kanban (literally "billboard" or "signboard," [URL: Kanban]) is a scheduling system for lean production and shares a number of similarities with Scrum. In a software development context, it is described as a project and change management approach to IT projects [Anderson 10]. Its basic principles come from lean management theory [URL: Lean] and are designed to visualize and optimize the flow of work within a value-added chain. Kanban is based on three key components:

Project and change management methodologies

- **The Kanban Board:**
  The process is visualized using cards (or "tickets") on a board. The individual steps in the process are represented by columns and the task by cards that are moved across the board from left to right as each task progresses.

- **Work-in-Progress (WIP) Limit:**
  The number of current tasks (Work in Progress, or WIP) is limited by the number of tickets allowed for each process step (or by limiting the number of tickets the board can hold). If any part of the production line has excess capacity, it pulls a ticket from an earlier stage in the process. This approach illustrates the use of "pull" rather than "push" methodology.

- **Lead Time:**
  Kanban is used to optimize the continuous flow of tasks by minimizing the (average) lead time for the complete value stream.

Scrum works in a similar fashion, using a whiteboard to provide a transparent, visual model of progress for the individual tasks within the process. Tasks that are not currently being actioned are maintained in the Backlog and are transferred to the whiteboard as soon as additional capacity becomes available.

Unlike Scrum, Kanban is not iterative and has no equivalent concept to Sprints[11]. Kanban is designed to *continually* optimize the production process and to reduce the overall time required to produce a complete

Kanban does not use iterations and Sprints.

---

11. As iterations are not forbidden, Kanban can be used iteratively, managing iterations of varied lenght.

product—in other words, it ensures a steady throughput (or flow) of tasks. A Kanban process allows you to ship its deliverables item by item. The produced items do not necessarily constitute a release. Timeboxing and its associated effort estimation are not needed as part of the Kanban model. In contrast, Scrum is designed to deliver a complete product at predefined intervals, so the end of a Sprint automatically synchronizes all the current tasks and delivers a potentially shippable product.

Scrum vs. Kanban
    The differences outlined above make it clear that Scrum is a good choice for producing software packages release by release whereas Kanban fits to efficiently manage the production of more or less independent items.

    For example, the Kanban model can be used to increase the efficiency of an IT support team, with each support enquiry representing a Kanban ticket. [Anderson 10] cites a software maintenance team that produces patches as an example of a valid Kanban approach. The team's goal is to produce individual patches and make them available to the customer as quickly as possible. Each patch represents an independent one-person programming job, making Kanban the ideal project management model.

Case Study 2–2

> **The eHome Controller Project 2-2: Using Kanban to Develop Adapters**
>
> The new Scrum Master invites all the members of the Scrum Team, all other hardware and software developers and the support team to a meeting to explain the new methodology. The meeting introduces the team to both Scrum and Kanban methods.
>
> The resulting discussion debates whether Scrum or Kanban is the more appropriate approach and whether Kanban might be suitable for implementation in other teams. It becomes apparent that the support team's ticket-based system already includes some elements of the Kanban model but could nonetheless benefit from introducing other elements, such as WIP limits.
>
> Because adapters can be developed in isolation, the team considers whether the development of new adapters can be better managed using Scrum or Kanban. Individual adapters are not dependent on each other and rarely have a significant effect on the system as a whole. In principle, a new or updated adapter can be integrated into the system at any time, making a strict Sprint-driven development cycle unnecessary. The team decides to take a closer look at Kanban as soon as the task of adapter development turns up in the Product Backlog.

2.3   **Traditional Process Models**

Traditional process models divide a project into distinct phases designed to achieve predefined milestones. They also define roles that assign tasks to specific members of the project team.

As well controlling timing, the phases of a traditional project also define the various levels of abstraction on which the system being developed is viewed. The widely used V-Model is a particularly good example of this approach:

Project phases as levels of abstraction

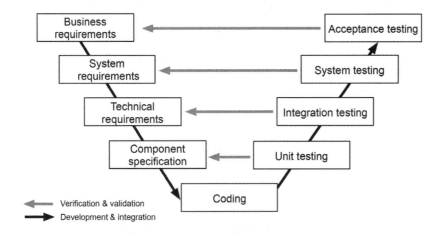

Fig. 2–3
Levels of abstraction and test phases of the V-Model

"The left-hand branch of the diagram symbolizes the increasingly complex steps involved in designing, developing and programming the desired system, while the right-hand branch shows the integration and testing steps necessary to assemble the individual building blocks into a complete functioning system. Integration and testing ends with validation" [Spillner/ Linz 14, Section 3.1]. This step also involves producing a set of documents and/or artifacts that completely describes the system at the current level of abstraction. This approach to software development is thus predominantly document-based.

Phases vs. Sprints

The Scrum approach is different. It views all levels of abstraction simultaneously during every Sprint and develops the entire system incrementally. The requirements are altered as necessary, code is rewritten, and the system architecture and appropriate tests are optimized at each step along the way. The volume of documentation is reduced to a minimum for each iteration and direct communication and discussion between all those involved takes its place.

Project management
and planning

Traditional project management techniques plan the various aspects of the project (aims, time constraints, costs and resources) as precisely as possible in advance and conduct the project in such a way that the plan as it stands is fulfilled, from start to finish.

The project manager uses the proposed structure of the project to create a plan that includes all the planned tasks and their interdependencies and sets them up within an appropriate timeframe. The time and resources required to execute the entire project are estimated in advance. If we were to plan our eHome Controller project using traditional methods, the initial plan might look something like the one shown in case study 2-3:

Case Study
eHome Controller 2–3:
A traditional plan for the
eHome Controller
project

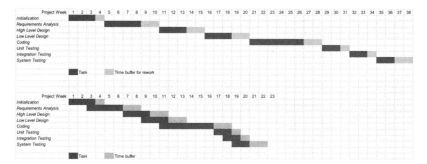

Weaknesses of traditional
project-planning methods

The inherent weaknesses of this approach are obvious:

- Early tasks, such as project initialization, are planned clearly but often in too much detail in comparison to the rest of the plan. Early phases of the project are often allocated more resources than necessary.
- Because the necessary input (for example, the design of the user interface or the required bus protocols) is often only available once the project has started, the effort estimation necessary to accurately allocate time isn't always sufficiently precise. Such a plan therefore allows for the time allocated by management rather than the time actually required by the team. This means that the planned deadlines are often subject to uncertainty.
- In order to account for the originally defined aim of "Release #1 ready in three months," the project manager has also drafted a backup plan that sees completion of a first release after five months' work. The trick used here was to reckon without the necessary time buffer.
- The content of the individual phases is not clearly defined. The project manager has to ensure that she or he and the team have a precise idea of the aim of each phase before it begins. On the other hand, a degree of

imprecision gives management the necessary leeway to absorb planning errors and potential deviations from the original plan.

- The assumption that QA will discover errors and defects is covered by buffer time allocated to reworking. At this stage, it is unclear whether two weeks' reworking time will be too little or too much. In any case, reworking relates to local corrections within the affected milestone. There is no time budget for any reworking of prior phases that may be affected.

- A lot of time can pass before the product can be comprehensively tested and delivered. In our example, 20 or 38 weeks will pass between the end of the design phase and the first integration test, which means that delivery can take place after five or nine months at the earliest.

Even if the initial plan is realistic and error-free, all aspects of the plan (tasks, timing, resources etc.) are subject to change in the course of the project. Even the most carefully laid plan can quickly become outdated, requiring time-consuming adjustment and replanning. At its worst, traditional project management can be seen as a constant losing battle with unforeseen but unavoidable change.

Scrum solves this conundrum by doing without an overall project plan and instead using the agile management tools listed earlier. Nevertheless, the work environment can make it necessary to define a plan for Scrum projects too. For example, a milestone or time budget that covers multiple Sprints can be a useful aid to planning long-term contractual obligations with customers, suppliers, colleagues or other parallel projects. If additional resources are required it can be helpful (or necessary) to be able to justify them. In such cases, it helps to have a written allocation of resources based on systematic effort estimation.

Scrum projects require planning too.

Iterative (incremental) development helps to counteract the weaknesses listed above and is thus a widely used aspect of traditional process models.

Iterative models, too, define various project phases but explicitly[12] allow for the repetition (iteration) of specific phases or combinations of phases. An iteration serves to enable the correction of flaws or errors by repeating a phase, or to expand its goals (i.e., to create a new product increment). The Rational Unified Process created by the Rational Software

Iterative development

---

12. A project manager can repeat (i.e., iterate) a phase of a linear model, too. There are many good reasons for doing so, but these all (strictly speaking) represent a deviation from the linear approach.

Corporation (a division of IBM) [URL: RUP] is a widely used iterative process model.

Iterative development processes are often wrongly considered to be the same as agile development processes. A Scrum Sprint can include any type of task, from improvements to system architecture to implementation and testing of individual features. In contrast, traditional project phases encapsulate tasks of a particular type (draft system architecture, for example). The Scrum stipulation that every Sprint (i.e., every iteration) should produce a potentially shippable product is not an inherent component of iterative development in general.

In other words, an iteration in a traditionally planned project isn't the equivalent of a Scrum Sprint. Any iterative developer who wishes to switch to Scrum has to understand and allow for this fundamental difference. Iterations within an Extreme Programming (XP) environment are also different from Sprints. XP produces a shippable product using a variable number of iterations, which means that the set of tasks covered by a single iteration can vary too—from system redesign through refactoring to the design and implementation of new features.

Incremental development   Incremental development is the most widely used development process in use today. It delivers product with varying stages of development at regular intervals. Iterative development is a prerequisite of incremental development and the process that results is often referred to as a combination of the two.

The intervals at which increments (i.e., releases) are produced varies from process model to process model. Traditional models foresee releases at half-yearly or yearly (and in some cases even longer) intervals. Agile processes radically shorten the release cycle. Scrum stipulates that every Sprint produces a new release that can be shipped if necessary. In practice, the process differentiates between internal release candidate (RC) versions and real releases. Many Scrum projects aim to produce a new release every three months by way of monthly Sprints. Teams that have perfected the art of continuous integration (see chapter 5) and, as a result, practice continuous delivery (CD) are often capable of deploying product on a daily basis. However, CD assumes that deployment takes place in a fully automated, controlled environment as found in some companies' internal IT systems and in many Web and eCommerce environments. Such systems can be kept current by way of nightly deployment.

2.4 Comparing Process Models

Differentiating between project management, human resource management, development techniques and quality management is a useful way to visualize the differences between the above-listed process models.

Fig. 2–4

*The major aspects of
a process model*

Each model deals with these aspects with varying intensity and using different philosophies and methods:

- **Scrum** is an empirical, adaptive approach to project management. It replaces comprehensive planning with the ability to react quickly, flexibly and appropriately to project events. Scrum does not require the use of specific development techniques, although XP is often favored. Product quality is ensured by the team's know-how and consistent use of the agreed development techniques. The team is responsible for its own success and, ideally, works with a team leader who has no overriding authority. Predefined routines (for example, Sprint Retrospectives) ensure that continual optimization takes place at project level.

- **Kanban** is an approach to task management that is designed for use in permanent workgroups or departments rather than in individual projects. It does not require the use of specific techniques. The team works within a joint value chain in which each team member has his/her own specific function. Product quality is ensured by the skills of the team members and immediate error correction. Predefined routines (for example, Retrospectives) ensure that continual optimization takes place.

▪ **Traditional models** are based on a pre-planned, deterministic project management approach. The team works according to instructions given by the project manager, who is considered to be the team members' superior. The project manager is responsible for monitoring progress and initiating any required corrective measures. The techniques used depend on the structure of the underlying plan and company-specific regulations (e.g., specific protocols or proprietary quality management systems). Continuous optimization is usually part of the project plan and is implemented by way of the quality management system and regular internal or external audits.

Table 2-1 illustrates the most important differences between process models.

Tab. 2-1

Comparing process models

		Scrum	Kanban	Traditional
Project Management	**Product planning**	Product vision, Roadmap, Product Backlog	–	Roadmap
	Project planning	Product Backlog	–	Project plan with milestones
	Task planning	Sprint Backlog for each iteration	Backlog	Specific phases
	Iteration	Predefined iteration duration (Sprints)	Continuous	According to project plan
	Iteration duration	Typically 1-4 weeks	–	According to project plan
	Status monitoring	Daily with the entire team, on a whiteboard	Daily with the entire team, on a whiteboard	By project manager, based on milestones
	Timeboxing	Yes	No	Project manager decides
	Delivery	Following each iteration (i.e., at the end of every Sprint)	Continually with the completion of each task	With each release or upon completion of project
	Change management	Via Backlog-update	Via Backlog-update	Via existing change management system
	Metrics	Burndown chart	Work in Progress (WIP)	Adhesion to deadlines, Effort, Costs

Quality Management	**Process optimization**	Project review, inspect and adapt (bottom-up)	Kaizen	Internal and external audits (e.g., according to ISO 9001), Process optimization programs (top-down)
	Verification/ Testing	Continuous within the Sprint	Per task	Testing against project specifications during test phases
	Validation/ Approval	User demo at the end of a Sprint (fulfillment of acceptance criteria)	Per task according to predefined criteria	Acceptance test at project completion
Development Tools	**Techniques**	Common but not obligatory: Pair Programming[a], Continuous Integration (CI)[b], Test First Programming[c], Incremental Design[d], Clean Code[e], Refactoring[f]	No specific stipulations	Depends on the model in use. Some include predefined coding, tooling guidelines etc.
Human Resources	**Values and principles**	Agile Manifest, Scrum Values: Commitment, - Focus, Openess, Respect, Courage	Kaizen, Lean Management, Agile Manifest	Project management, process model, continuous optimization (ISO 9000)
	Organization	Scrum Team, -Product Owner, Scrum Master		Team leader, project management, project organization
	Training	On own initiative, desire to improve, learning with the team	Learning with the team	Company training plan, human resources development
	Allocation of work	Interdisciplinary (cross-functional)	Specialists work on each stage of the process	Highly specialized

a. From XP: "Write all production code with two people sitting at one machine" [Beck/ Andres 04, p. 42].

b. From XP: "Integrate and test changes after no more than a couple of hours" [Beck/ Andres 04, p. 49].

c. From XP: "Write a failing automated test before changing any code" [Beck/Andres 04, p. 50].

d. From XP: "Invest in the design of the system every day" [Beck/Andres 04, p. 51].

e.   "We'll know how to write good code. And we'll know how to transform bad code into good code" [Martin 08, p. 2].

f.   "For each few lines of code we add, we pause and reflect on the new design. Did we just degrade it? If so we clean it up ..." [Martin 08, p. 172].

3 Planning an Agile Project

This chapter describes the lightweight project management tools that Scrum uses in place of a traditional project plan. It is aimed primarily at readers who wish to make the switch to agile development, but nevertheless contains plenty of comments and tips on the error prevention that using agile planning tools can provide.

Agile project management is based on the assumption that the team learns from every Sprint. Poor decisions can be examined and corrected in subsequent Sprints and the team can react quickly to changes in the project's environment. Each new product increment that a Sprint produces gives the team and the customer new insights into the product's true requirements. Of course, each increment can also generate new and better ideas regarding the product's functionality and how it can be most elegantly implemented.

The team should continually evaluate these experiences and include all new ideas that add value in the Product Backlog. This means that the best ideas can be immediately incorporated in the form of new tasks in the plan for the next Sprint.

This adaptive, empirical approach to project planning makes the development process extremely flexible, and constant learning is an automatic part of the process. It also means that the team is always able to react swiftly to changes in the customer's requirements and the overall project environment.

Adaptive, empirical planning

The ability to change direction in every new Sprint doesn't mean that the team works aimlessly. Even in a Scrum environment, reactive work practices alone will not result in a successful project. A Scrum Team also needs objectives that look beyond just the current Sprint. The following sections outline the instruments you can use to give a Scrum Team direction.

3.1 Product Vision

The product vision describes concisely and accurately how the finished product should look and what it needs to be capable of. The shorter and more concise the product vision, the better chance you will have of creating the desired product. It can take the form of a sketch on a flipchart, a list of the top 10 features required by the customer or a picture of a competitor's product that the team aims to beat.

The Product Backlog *is not suited for use as* *a product vision.*   The Product Backlog (see section 3.3) is usually too detailed to double as the product vision, and too many Backlog items can make the project goal less clear. Ideally, the product vision serves to help prioritize the Backlog items and separate significant items from less relevant ones. The eHome team ended up drafting the following vision:

Case Study 3–1

> **The eHome Controller Project 3-1: Product Vision**
>
> The Product Owner invites the development team to a workshop to discuss the project and develop a vision based on management targets and the customer's own requirements.
> The system has to work on smartphones and other mobile devices and needs to support existing third-party devices as well as any new ones that are due to hit the market soon. The Product Owner and the team draft the following goals:
>
> ▪ Browser-based user interface: This means that the owner of an eHome can control its systems via a PC, smartphone or tablet without having to install any additional software.
> ▪ Clear, simple handling: All rooms and the devices in them are to be represented by individual icons or photos uploaded by the user. The interface shouldn't appear too technical and must be comprehensible for users who don't have experience using IT-based systems.
> ▪ Manufacturer independent: The Controller must support actuators and sensors from various manufacturers, and the appropriate bus protocols.

3.2 Architecture Vision

Once the product vision has been drafted, the team can begin to consider how to turn it into reality. The first step in the process is to draft an architecture vision, which contains an overview of the product and its individual components. Based on the product vision outlined above, the eHome team designs the basic architecture shown in the schematic as in case study 3-2-diagramm[1].

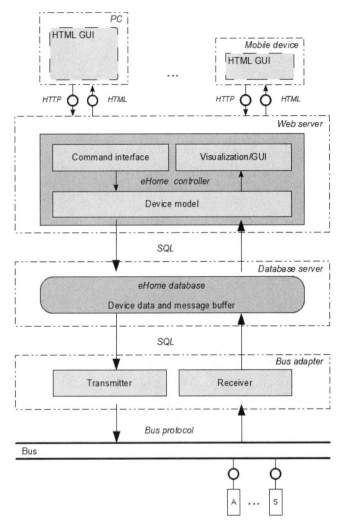

Case Study
eHome Controller 3–2:
The eHome Controller
project architecture

Like the product vision, the architecture vision doesn't have to be too detailed, and a simple sketch of the main components can suffice. The architecture schematic doesn't have to take the form of an UML diagram or any other type of formal notation as long as all members of the team (including the Product Owner and the Scrum Master) understand it.

1.　Notation based on FMC [URL: FMC].

Architecture vision as a guideline for coding and testing

Like the product vision, the architecture vision acts as a guide to the Product Backlog and the ensuing Sprints. It helps to provide a sustainable project overview that doesn't have to be rejigged before every Sprint and also helps to draft meaningful sets of tasks that can be intelligently distributed among the team and the upcoming Sprints.

The architecture vision also lays important testing foundations from a very early stage by defining the most important product components and their system interfaces as foreseeable test objects. This way, testing and other quality assurance measures can be aligned with the evolving system right from the very first Sprint.

Emergent architecture

Even if the team drafts the system architecture and the accompanying schematic at an early stage, this doesn't mean that it cannot be changed later. The system architecture can and should be revised and adjusted regularly during the following Sprints. Findings from the continuing implementation and feedback from product demos may need to be worked into the overall architecture. Adjusting a logically designed architecture step by step is clearly a much more productive approach than simply having programmers code a random set of classes that don't adhere to a clear plan.

3.3 Product Backlog

The Product Owner uses the Product Backlog to collect and prioritize all the requirements that are or may be due for inclusion in the finished product. However, the Product Backlog is not a project plan and is not a to-do list. It serves instead as a kind of notepad for ideas that are thrown up during development. The entries are prioritized according to their relevance and the potential value they add to the product, although even these priorities are not binding with regard to if and when an entry actually gets implemented. The Product Owner for the eHome Controller project drafted the following Product Backlog and prioritized it according to estimated business value[2] to the overall project:

---

2. Prioritization doesn't precisely define or determine the desired order of completion. The team can choose requirements according to the basic order of prioritization and thus remain flexible while planning the Sprint.

Topic	Priority	Description / *Acceptance criteria*
Control and Monitoring		As an eHome owner I want to control all connected devices and monitor all data collected by the sensors simply and centrally:
	2	☐ *The GUI displays the current status of all connected actuators and sensors*
	1	☐ *Actuator: Clicking its icon triggers the actuator's switching function*
	2	☐ *Sensor: Clicking its icon transmits the sensor's data and displays it*
Bus Adapter		As an eHome owner, I want the system to support devices from various manufacturers, making me manufacturer-independent:
	1	☐ *A bus adapter translates controller signals into ones that can be processed by the appropriate third-party protocol*
	1	☐ *All eHome Tools devices can be controlled via the eHome Tools Adapter*
Device Control		As an eHome owner, I want to control various classes of device (e.g., lamps, dimmers, blinds) but, in order to avoid faulty operation, the controller only allows commands for each class of device to be executed by that device.
		As an eHome user I can:
	1	☐ *Switch connected lamps on and off*
	3	☐ *Adjust the brightness of each lamp from 0-100% using a dimmer*
	2	☐ *Open and close blinds or adjust them to a certain angle*
GUI		I want to control the system using a browser-based interface so that no additional software is required.
		The GUI runs in the following PC browser:
	1	☐ *Firefox version 15.0 and later*
GUI-Icons	2	Each class of device is represented by its own icon. This makes it simple to identify the right device and looks cool.
Switch Programming	3	All devices can be programmed to automate regular routines. For example, to tilt all blinds at 7am on weekdays, open all south-facing blinds at 8:30am and close all blinds at 8:30pm.

Case Study
eHome Controller 3–3:
The initial Product Backlog for the eHome Controller project

Like all other Scrum-based planning documents, the Product Backlog changes from Sprint to Sprint. New ideas and requirements are added, priorities are altered, obsolete requirements are deleted, single items are grouped in clusters, and rough ideas are refined and divided into smaller, better-defined tasks. The Product Owner is responsible for maintaining the Product Backlog, while the Scrum Master ensures that the Backlog is kept according to the basic rules of the Scrum process. In our example, the Scrum Master notes that the last two items in the Backlog have no acceptance criteria and asks the Product Owner to draft these too (see section 3.9.3).

Testers help draft approval criteria

In order to draft the right approval criteria, the team's testers need to be involved in the process. This also makes it easier for the testers to design appropriate acceptance tests later on.

3.4 Story Map

Based on the product and architecture visions and the Product Backlog, the Product Owner can create a story map with the team that maps the goals of the coming Sprints. A Sprint's goal can be an important requirement or a cluster of requirements that form an overriding theme for a Sprint. Goals designed to improve the process itself can also serve as Sprint Goals. The eHome team created the following story map for its first three Sprints:

Case Study
eHome Controller 3–4:
The eHome team's initial story map

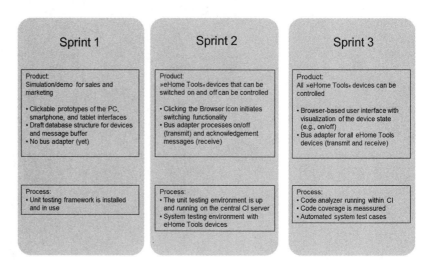

However, a story map is only ever a statement of intent. The team does not guarantee that the goals it contains will be tackled or reached. The goals and the Sprints they are allocated to can change due to customer feedback or to the increasing expertise of the team.

A story map
is not obligatory.

When the Product Owner discusses the story map with the customer, it has to be made clear that it does not imply a concrete commitment to the inclusion of particular features in a specific release. Such commitments, in whatever form, undermine the agile approach and would quickly force the team to return to a traditional, incremental development process.

Although the Product Owner doesn't guarantee when the product will reach a particular stage in its development, an agile story map still has certain advantages over a traditional project roadmap:

Advantages of a story map
compared with a traditional
roadmap

- The sales team and the Product Owner promise no deadlines that the development team might not be able to stick to. Development teams in traditional projects often regard such deadlines as unrealistic anyway. If they are not managed strictly, projects quickly get behind schedule and the sales team will have to revise its roadmap accordingly. An agile story map is the stress-free alternative and, in the end, achieves the same goals as a traditional roadmap.
- In addition to hearing about the development priorities within the team, the customer is given a realistic overview of the scheduled features and the timeframe within which they will be completed. This approach also enables the customer to see any favored features in context and can thus give useful feedback with regard to which version(s) of the story map he/she can best live with.
- The customer is able to actively influence feature priorities. The team can also analyze the requirements and priorities of various customer and user groups and include these in its own prioritization process.
- The manufacturer has more leeway to soak up the conflicts of interest that may result from a change in priority and the allocation of a feature to an earlier or later Sprint. Traditional projects are often less flexible because a particular roadmap has been promised to the customer, and such promises are difficult or impossible to revoke or revise.

3.5   Sprint Backlog

During the Sprint Planning meeting at the start of each Sprint, the team identifies and pulls the items from the Product Backlog that are to be completed in the course of the upcoming Sprint into the Sprint Backlog. These include all the tasks and requirements necessary to reach the Sprint Goal stipulated in the story map.

The "pull" principle   The team makes sure that it doesn't allocate more tasks than it can deal with in the course of the Sprint. In other words, the team itself uses the "pull" principle to determine what it can achieve. To ensure that this process works, the team has to precisely estimate the effort involved in every task—a process that is also conducted within the team as part of the Planning Poker.

Planning Poker   Each team member estimates how much effort each of the planned tasks will involve. Once all team members have given their estimates, an average value is calculated for each task[3]. If estimates differ significantly, the team has to consider whether the task has been correctly interpreted by everyone involved, and needs to rectify any anomalies before re-estimating the required effort. This approach ensures that the resulting estimates are accurate.

Unlike a traditional project plan in which the project leader stipulates in advance which tasks have to be completed by which deadlines, the Sprint Backlog represents a commitment by the team to the Product Owner to complete the Sprint and its allotted tasks within the scheduled timeframe[4]. This commitment is the tradeoff for being allowed to choose the tasks and estimate the time necessary to complete them. The team can only make this commitment if it is given the necessary planning freedom.

Potentially shippable product   A successful Sprint delivers a potentially shippable product. Early Sprints should deliver at least a prototype to show the customer, while later Sprints should generate constantly improving releases that can be used in a productive environment. The commitment to delivering shippable product has various consequences, especially for the quality assurance (QA) and testing aspects of a Scrum project:

---

3.   To prevent rogue estimates from spoiling the results, the median value is often used in place of the arithmetic mean.

4.   Individual tasks can be redrafted during the Sprint if the team thinks this will make the Sprint Goal easier to achieve.

- The features implemented in the course of a Sprint have to be tested, which means that all QA work and testing schedules have to be planned as part of the Sprint. There is no separate test phase that takes place once the Sprint is over.
- Promised features have to work! This means that all other required components, such as drivers and the GUI, have to be present and must mesh perfectly with the new feature. The product itself is built "vertically" rather than in horizontal layers that correspond to the layers of the system architecture (as is often the case in traditionally managed projects).
- The team risks coding too many generic features. Of course, every project architecture contains generic functions and class libraries that reduce the amount of effort involved in implementation. This only becomes a problem if too many classes are generated with a view to supporting future use cases. Many projects end up using only 10-30% of the available generic functions, which means that the time spent coding the other 70-90% was wasted. Additionally, there is no usable feedback available for unused code. It is therefore very important to make sure that class libraries are only developed far enough to support the parts of the system that are involved in the current Sprint.
- A task is only complete when its Definition of Done (DoD) criteria have been fulfilled. This means that every task is followed by additional steps (such as a code review, drafting new tests, test automation, updating documentation etc.) that are often overlooked or performed later in traditionally managed projects. All of these extra tasks have to be taken into account (either explicitly or implicitly as part of the "done" criteria) when planning a Sprint. In turn, this increases the amount of effort required to complete a task and reduces the net number of features that can be addressed in the course of the Sprint. However, it does ensure that the features in question really are done by the time the Sprint is over.

3.6   Team Charter

Traditionally managed projects currently envisage the creation of a QA plan according to IEEE 730 and an overall testing plan (possibly with additional test level plans) according to IEEE 829. These plans are used as the basis for the work that follows. Both QA and test plans can be heavy, multi-page documents and their content often differs widely from the real-world project that ensues. Basic components (such as project organization, processes and conventions, and scheduling) that are required parts of the standards mentioned above[5] no longer require individual attention in Scrum-based projects since they are already an integral part of the Scrum framework. However, other aspects of planning, such as supplier management, testing strategies and test infrastructure, do not automatically become obsolete just because a project team is using Scrum.

Using IEEE 730 and IEEE 829 as checklists

As long as a project is not subject to regulations that require standardized planning (see section 7.3), a Scrum project can easily do without both these plans and can instead use the tenets of the standards as checklists. The Scrum Master uses them as part of the retrospectives to determine whether requirements from these standards are relevant to the project at hand. Where regulation is seen as necessary, the team drafts its own rules, which are then recorded in a Team Charter. The Charter also includes rules for testing and QA (see chapter 7). The major difference between a Team Charter and traditional QA documentation is that it contains no externally drafted rules that are forced on the team. Instead, like the Sprint Backlog, it represents a voluntary commitment on the part of the team. Because these rules are voluntary and are often based on known agile practices, they are usually simple and concise. The eHome team drafted the following rules:

Case Study
eHome Controller 3–5:
The eHome Controller project Team Charter

Team Charter
– How we will implement Scrum in the eHome Controller project –

Sprint
- Duration: 4 weeks
- Each Sprint is preceded by a Sprint Planning phase and ends with a review

Meetings
- Daily Scrum: At 11am, maximum duration 15 minutes, Product Owner takes part
- Sprint Planning: Wednesday at 9am (at the start of the Sprint), maximum duration 1 day
- Review: Tuesday at 11am (at the end of the Sprint)

Practices
- Planning Poker:
  - Estimation in Story Points (SP), minimum of 1, maximum of 13 SPs per task
  - Break complex tasks down into smaller units
  - Acceptance criteria are to be agreed on and recorded in writing

---

5.   Chapter 7 goes into more detail on the content and structure of these types of plans.

3.7   Test Planning and Test Management

3.7.1   Traditional Test Management

In traditional projects managed using the V-Model, the test manager usually has the following responsibilities:

- Organizing the test: Planning and sourcing of the required resources (staff, infrastructure, tools), team organization and ensuring that appropriate skills are available.
- Defining test strategy: Goals, objects, selecting appropriate methods, defining start and end criteria, effort and cost estimation, risk assessment and continual development of test strategy according to results and project progress.
- Defining test content: Content, scope and prioritization.
- Test management: Allocate testing tasks and coordinate them with ongoing development, monitor progress using appropriate metrics, analyze and communicate results.
- Consulting: Assist project management with QA issues and help decide when to release a product.

Thus, a traditional test manager fills two main roles:

- Organizing and leading the test team(s) as a project lead responsible for the subproject "testing."
- Planning what gets tested (and how) in the role of a software testing expert.

3.7.2   Test Management in Scrum

A Scrum Team is a self-organizing, cross-functional team that does not work under the authority of a project manager. Scrum gives responsibility for all work to the entire team. Coding and testing take place within the same team and are not treated separately.

Consequently, a Scrum Team has no dedicated test manager and distributes the responsibilities associated with this role within the team.

A Scrum Team has no dedicated test manager.

Organizing the test is the responsibility of the Scrum Master. If test tools or infrastructure require improvement or replacement, or if the necessary skills are not available within the team, the Scrum Master is responsible for ensuring that these impediments are remedied.

The overall management role is covered by basic Scrum practices, and testing tasks are either scheduled explicitly as tasks within a Sprint or implicitly as part of the done criteria of other tasks. The monitoring and analysis of testing progress and results are part of the highly automated continuous integration aspect of Scrum (see section 5.5), making manual test monitoring almost completely redundant and the traditional test manager role superfluous.

In theory, Scrum expects the entire team to be responsible for defining test strategy and content (see above). However, software testing requires specialist skills, and testing experience is necessary if the team is to make the right decisions.

The team requires a member with dedicated testing expertise.

For these reasons, the team should contain at least one appropriately qualified full-time member who is dedicated to testing[6]. This person is then responsible for designing appropriate risk-oriented tests and implementing them in all Sprints. This role also includes advising the Product Owner on QA and product release issues. There is no reason not to call this role the Scrum Team's test manager, and independent test specialists who offer methodical support are often a good choice for the job.

Defect management

Defect management plays only a minor role in agile project management scenarios. This is because most defects can be reproduced at will using automated test routines, all team members work in constant close cooperation[7] and are generally already aware of any defects or coding issues, and ideally, all defects are remedied as soon as they are discovered. The combination of these factors means that entering a defect in a defect management system doesn't usually add any value to the process. The person responsible for fixing the defect knows about it already, so there is no need to record it for later attention. However, even Scrum doesn't always produce such an ideal scenario, making it necessary to implement a tool-based defect management system[8]. A defect is entered into the system if:

- It is discovered during manual testing (or some other routine) rather than by the usual automated test systems. In this case, registering the defect is necessary if it is to be reproduced.

---

6. The international accepted standard is the ISTQB* Certified Tester program. See section 7.7 for more details.
7. Based on XP primary practices, such as Sit Together and Pair Programming (see [Beck/Andres 04]).
8. Requirements for defect management and the structure of defect reports are outlined in IEEE 829, IEEE 1044, ISO/IEC/IEEE 29119-2.

- It requires further analysis or handling that involves additional (internal or external) resources. In this case, documenting the defect ensures that all relevant people are informed. (This is often the case during integration and system tests.)
- It cannot or should not be remedied during the current Sprint. This ensures that the error isn't forgotten.

3.7.3   Test Levels in Scrum

In Scrum-based projects, it is necessary to conduct tests at all the same levels as you would in a traditional V-Model project (seer fig. 2-3). These various test levels are based on varying technical requirements and pursue different objectives and thus require the application of differing test methods and specialist know-how.

The testing principles established in the V-Model are just as relevant in agile projects:

The principles of the V-Model still apply.

- Programming and testing activities (represented by the left- and right-hand sides of the V) are equally important to the success of the project.
- Tests conducted on a particular level serve to check the product at a specific level of abstraction.
- Tests can serve either to validate (i.e., have we developed the right product?) or verify (i.e., have we developed the product right?).

However, in a Scrum-based project, these test phases are not performed sequentially, but instead take place parallel to one another within each Sprint, ideally on a daily basis! Chapters 4, 5, and 6 outline in detail how this approach works.

Test phases run in parallel rather than sequentially.

3.8   Introducing Agile Planning

If you are introducing Scrum into a team for the first time, or are starting a new Scrum project, the Scrum Master has to make sure that the Product Owner begins by developing the product vision, the architecture vision and the story map together with the team. In all three cases, conciseness is much more important than the level of detail:

- A list of the ten most important product features is more useful than a lengthy specification sheet.
- A clear sketch of the planned system architecture is more useful than a sophisticated UML diagram.

▨ Allocating top priority themes and tasks to the next three Sprints is more useful than attempting to allocate the entire contents of the Backlog to a complete sequence of future Sprints.

It is essential that the person who maintains the Backlog checks regularly that all tasks relevant to the product and the work of the team are incorporated into the Backlog.

Preventing the creation of a shadow Backlog

Otherwise, the team members will quickly develop shadow Backlogs made up of private to-do lists. If some members of the team work part-time or on other projects, the Sprint plan has to account for the resulting resource shortfall. For example, a team member who is also responsible for answering customer support calls cannot be budgeted with 100% capacity for a Sprint. The team must not be allowed to speculate that fewer support calls than usual will crop up during a Sprint.

Finally, the Scrum Master has to ensure that testing work doesn't get neglected or forgotten.

3.9 Questions and Exercises

3.9.1 Self-Assessment

Questions and exercises to help you assess how agile your project or team really is.

1. Are the product and architecture visions for my product/project defined? What are they?
2. Who compiled these documents? Who maintains them?
3. Is the Product Backlog well organized? How is it structured? Who maintains it?
4. Which criteria are used to prioritize Backlog items?
5. Do we have an overall plan that covers more than just the next three Sprints? Are we using a story map? To what degree are the existing plans binding?
6. Is the Sprint Backlog well organized? Is it well structured?
7. Who maintains the Sprint Backlog? Who is allowed to edit Backlog items? Is the Sprint protected against change while active?
8. What is the team's Definition of Done?
9. Is there a Team Charter? If not, who defines the team's rules of engagement and how?

10. How do we deal with test management? Do we have a dedicated test manager? Who fulfills the test management role?
11. Which different test levels have we defined and which do we use?

3.9.2   Methods and Techniques

These questions will help you to review the content of the current chapter.

1. What is the purpose of the architecture vision?
2. What is the difference between the Product Backlog and the Sprint Backlog?
3. What is the purpose of the story map?
4. Why do we have to precisely estimate the effort involved in all planned tasks when planning a Sprint?
5. What does it mean when we say that a Sprint is protected?
6. How are test and QA tasks represented in the Sprint Backlog?
7. What is the purpose of the Team Charter?

3.9.3   Other Exercises

These exercises will help you delve deeper into topics touched on in the course of the chapter.

1. Explain which aspects of the architecture vision and the planned product architecture influence Sprint Planning.
2. Draft the additional acceptance criteria missing in figure 3-3.
3. Design the test(s) you would use to determine whether the product fulfills these criteria.
4. To which level of the V-Model would you allocate these tests?

4 Unit Testing and Test First

This chapter explains what unit testing is and how it can be automated. It is aimed at system testers and testing specialists, as well as team members with little or no programming experience, and offers grass-roots information about developer-oriented testing techniques and tools. The material is designed to help you cooperate more closely with programmers and unit testers. There are also many tips that will help experienced unit testers improve their working methods. Based on these principles, we also introduce the Test First concept and explain its importance in an agile project management context.

4.1 Unit Testing

The term "unit testing" is often seen as a synonym for "developer testing" and serves to describe all the tests that developers apply to their software. The difference between the two approaches makes some sense in traditional projects that have separate integration and system testing teams, but is not applicable to Scrum projects in which all tasks are handled by the team as a whole. In a Scrum environment, it makes more sense to differentiate between the various objects that need to be tested.

The term "unit test"[1] describes all dynamic[2] tests that are used to check the functionality of a single, independent software component. According to [Spillner/Linz 14], the distinguishing characteristic of unit tests is that they are used to check components independently from other system components. This isolation serves to eliminate external influences

Unit tests check the internals of a single, independent component.

---

1. The ISTQB Glossary [URL: ISTQB Glossary] uses the term "component tests." However, "unit test" is still the most widely used term within the developer community.
2. A dynamic test is one that executes the object as part of the test. In contrast, static checks analyze the structure of an object but don't execute its code (see [Spillner/Linz 14]).

on the component in question. If a unit test reveals a defect, its source is sure to lie within the component being tested.

In non-object-oriented coding environments, functions, modules and scripts act as standalone components, whereas object-oriented programming sees classes and their associated methods as the smallest possible individual elements of a program that can be executed (and therefore tested) in isolation. Because object-oriented programming is the most common approach in use today, the following sections explains unit testing as applied to software classes[3].

4.1.1   Classes and Objects

A class consists of a set of variables (also known as attributes or properties) and a set of methods (also known as functions in some programming languages). Depending on their type, these variables can have different values assigned to them. Methods operate on the variables and manipulate their values.

However, a class itself is an abstract construct and only when it is executed does it create objects that exist in the memory of the computer that executes the code. These objects are instances of the predefined class whose behavior is determined by the methods associated with it. The values of the variables in an object determine its state at any given moment and an object can change its state over time if the values of its variables change. Thus, multiple objects created from the same class will usually have different states. The eHome Controller class Device[4] is a perfect example:

---

3.   The unit to be tested can consist of multiple basic components. All references to testing in this chapter can be equally well applied to simple or compound units.

4.   Like all code samples in this book, the sample class here is written in PHP. Although these represent full-fledged methods, PHP defines them using the function label. Variable identifiers start with a dollar sign $. The operator for accessing objects, variables and methods is ->. [Gutmans et al. 05] offers a fine introduction to PHP and [Schlossnagle 04] goes into more detail on more complex concepts. See also [URL: PHP]. (Unit) testing for PHP is explained in [Bergmann/Priebsch 11].

eHome Controller Case Study 4-1a: Class `Device`

The eHome Controller's GUI is designed to display the current switching state of every device currently attached to it (see the Product Backlog item "Control and Monitoring" in figure 3-3).

To fulfill this objective, the team programs a class called `Device`, in which every class object represents a specific device (for example, a particular lamp). The class has the variable `$status`, which describes the current status of the device in question. The methods `set_status()` and `get_status()` are used to change and read the current status:

```
class Device {// version 1
    public $name ='';
    public $status ='';
    public function __construct($my_name) {
        $this->name = $my_name;
    }
    public function set_status ($new_status) {
        $this->status = $new_status;
    }
    public function get_status () {
        return $this->status;
    }
}
```

This class exists as a singular piece of code within the eHome system but can be used to generate any number of device instances when run—for example, "kitchen light" or "hall power outlet"). All these objects behave in the same way, as determined by the `Device` class. Each device and thus, each device object, can nevertheless have its own individual status at any given moment. For example, the kitchen light is on while the power outlet in the hall is *off*.

These basic characteristics of classes and objects help us define the tasks required to test them. We have to make sure that the class itself functions properly for all potential object states, and the next two sections explain the appropriate test methods.

4.1.2 Testing the Methods of a Class

What approach do we need to take to unit test a class? An obvious answer would appear to be, "Every method the class contains." The eHome team writes a test class called `DeviceTest` to test the `Device` class.

Case Study 4–1b

eHome Controller Case Study 4-1b: Test class `DeviceTest`

```
include 'Device.php';                    // the class to be tested
class DeviceTest {                                    // version 1
    public function test_KitchenLightOn() {
        $device = new Device('kitchen light');         // setup
        $device->set_status('on');          // test procedure
        if ($device->status == 'on')               // check
            $myResult = TRUE;
        else    $myResult = FALSE;
        unset($device);                           // teardown
        return $myResult;
    }
}
$myTestSuite = new DeviceTest();
$myTestResult = $myTestSuite->test_KitchenLightOn();
                                        // execute test case
if ($myTestResult == TRUE)
    echo 'passed';
else    echo 'failed';
```

The `DeviceTest` class shown above contains just one simple test case called `test_KitchenLightOn` that serves to illustrate the principles involved in creating a unit test.

▨ Test cases are built according to a fixed pattern:

- **setup**: The test object is created or initialized. In our example, this is an object called `kitchen light`.
- **test procedure**: The actual testing steps are executed. In our example, the method `set_status()` is used to change the status of the `kitchen light` object to *on* and read the altered status.
- **check**: A comparison check is used to see whether the test was passed or failed. In this case, the test is designed to see whether the `set_status()` method functions correctly, so it simply checks whether the value of the variable `status` is the same as the one set using the `set_status()` method.
- **teardown**: Appropriate steps are then taken to return the system to its original state. This ensures that the test leaves the tested object as found. If you stick rigidly to this approach, the test cases remain independent from one another and you can perform all relevant

tests in any order. In our example, the kitchen light object created
to perform the test is deleted at the end of the routine[5].

▨ A test case serves to test one method only.

• If the **test procedure** and **check** sections are extended to include the
following commands, the second get_status() method can be
tested during the same run:

```
...
   $device = new Device('kitchen light');                    // setup
   $device->set_status('on');              // test procedure step 1
   $status_read = $device->get_status();   // test procedure step 2
   if ($status_read == 'on')                               // check
           $myResult = TRUE;
      else  $myResult = FALSE;
   unset($device);                                     // teardown
...
```

• If, however, the test fails and returns a failed value, the tester cannot
see whether set_status() or get_status() caused the failure. This
makes defect analysis more difficult. It is considered to be good
coding style to limit tests to checking only a single aspect of the
code's functionality.

When test_KitchenLightOn is executed, six of the eight lines of code that
make up the Device class are run, which is equivalent to 6/8=75% line coverage. The version that includes the get_status() test (using $status_read
= $device->get_status()) produces 100% line coverage! However, this is
due only to the simplicity of the Device class, and concluding that the test
object is correct would be a grave mistake. The Device class actually has
some significant deficiencies:

▨ The specifications of the variable $status say that it should display the
current switching state of a device using the values on and off. So far, so
good. Unfortunately, in its current form, $status can be allocated to
any other value too—for example, 30%, which doesn't make sense for a
power outlet. The Device class therefore has to ensure that $status can

<hr>

5. In fact, the teardown section shown here is not strictly necessary, as PHP automatically
deletes the test object when it exits the test_KitchenLightOn() method. Manual coding
of such garbage collection routines is only necessary in languages such as C or C++ that
don't do so automatically.

only be allocated the values on or off. This is achieved by adding an appropriate check to the set_status() method.

- Once this check has been built in, we also have to ensure that $status cannot be directly manipulated (i.e., by bypassing set_status()). All variables in this class are currently public, which means that even if the improved set_status() guarantees that $status can only have the values on or off, it is still possible to use $device->status='30%' to assign it an inadmissible status value. This means that the class could be assigned states that its methods cannot process or that are contrary to its planned functionality. We thus have to ensure that $status cannot be accessed directly by declaring its class variables as private.

- The variable $name is also public and needs to be declared private. Another weakness of $name is that it is set when an object is created using the class constructor __construct() but cannot subsequently be read. To do this, we need a method called get_name(). As soon as $name is declared private, the necessity of the method set_name() is called into question. The specifications are not clear on this point. Whether set_name() is necessary or not depends on the nature of the electrical appliances that we wish to control. If we assume that these devices are mobile, their names have to be flexible (for example, kitchen light might become hall light). If, however, kitchen light is used to define the lamp attached to the cable in the center of the kitchen ceiling, a constant name is perhaps a better representation of reality.

None of these shortcomings of the sample class Device are addressed or revealed by the unit test detailed above, which teaches us the following lessons:

- Line coverage of less than 100% proves that some test cases are missing. However, the converse argument is not valid—line coverage of 100% doesn't automatically mean that the test cases cover all eventualities.

- Even a unit test requires requirements- or specification-based test cases. If unit tests are designed on a white-box testing basis, it is impossible to tell whether specific requirements are wrongly interpreted or simply ignored.

- In order to check specific code attributes (for example, "all variables are private"), static code analysis or code review techniques are more appropriate than dynamic tests.

- The rule of thumb that states "every method needs to be tested" is worth noting, but one test case per method is not enough (except in the case of parameter-free methods). Even our relatively trivial method set_status()

requires at least four test cases to cover each of the values `'on'`, `'off'`, `'30%'` and `''`[6]. We need to identify a sufficient number of test cases for each method using equivalence partitioning and boundary value analysis[7].

These observations make it clear that the number of test cases required and the effort involved in applying them depends to a great degree on the design of the source code. Large numbers of parameters and complex nested conditions increase the amount of effort involved. During its code reviews, the team needs to check whether each method can be refactored to include fewer parameters and/or simplify any condition queries.

Code design and testing effort

Once these problems had been identified, the eHome team produced the following improved version of the Device class:

eHome Controller Case Study 4-2a: Improved Device class

Case Study 4–2a

```
class Device {                                    // version 2
    private $name;
    private $status;
    public function __construct($my_name) {
        $this->name = $my_name;
        $this->status = 'unknown';
    }
    public function get_name () {
        return $this->name;
    }
    public function set_status ($new_status) {
        if (is_validStatus($new_status)){
            $this->status = $new_status;
            return TRUE;
            }
        else return FALSE;
    }
    public function get_status () {
        return $this->status;
    }
    private function is_validStatus ($status) {
        if ($status=='on' OR $status=='off')
            return TRUE;
        else return FALSE;
    }
}
```

---

6. These represent the two valid values: an invalid value and a parameter that hasn't been set (i.e., an empty string).

7. These test design techniques are described in [Spillner/Linz 14].

The public methods in the new version of the class represent its API and therefore have to be covered by a sufficient number of test cases. As an exercise, check the line coverage that results if you run the test_Kitchen-LightOn case on the new version of Device (see also section 4.6.2). The team discussed this issue too, and coded a new version of DeviceTest as a result:

Case Study 4–2b

eHome Controller Case Study 4-2b: Improved test class DeviceTest

The programmer responsible for the test class added a test case to cover the status value '30%'. Because the variable $status (in the Device class) is now declared private, a test case can no longer poll $status directly and has to use the test object's API method getStatus() instead.

Version 2.1 of the class DeviceTest now contains two similar test cases that differ only in the content of their test procedure code. The programmer also improved the overall code quality by moving redundant code to a higher-level class called TestFrame[a]. Additional test cases for 'off' and '' have also been added. Version 2.2 of DeviceTest looks like this:

```
include 'Device.php';                    // the class to be tested
include 'TestFrame.php';   // simple home made Unit Test Framework
class DeviceTest extends TestFrame {              // version 2.2
    public function test_KitchenLightOn() {
        $device = new Device('kitchen light');            // setup
        $device->set_status('on');               // test procedure
        $this->assertEquals('on', $device->get_status(),
            'KitchenLightOn');                           // check
        unset($device);                              // teardown
    }
    public function test_KitchenLightOff() {
        $device = new Device('kitchen light');            // setup
        $device->set_status('off');              // test procedure
        $this->assertEquals('off', $device->get_status(),
            'KitchenLightOff');                          // check
        unset($device);                              // teardown
    }
    public function test_setStatusInvalid30() {
        $device = new Device('kitchen light');            // setup
        $device->set_status('30%');              // test procedure
        $this->assertEquals('unknown', $device->get_status(),
            'setStatusInvalid30');                       // check
        unset($device);                              // teardown
    }
```

a.   The source code for this and all other sample classes is available for download at the book's website [URL: SWT-knowledge].

```
    public function test_setStatusInvalidEmpty() {
        $device = new Device('kitchen light');           // setup
        $device->set_status('');                  // test procedure
        $this->assertEquals('unknown', $device->get_status(),
            'setStatusInvalidEmpty');                    // check
        unset($device);                            // teardown
    }
}
$myTestSuite = new DeviceTest();
$myTestSuite->test_KitchenLightOn();        // execute test case 1
$myTestSuite->test_KitchenLightOff();       // execute test case 2
$myTestSuite->test_setStatusInvalid30();    // execute test case 3
$myTestSuite->test_setStatusInvalidEmpty(); // execute test case 4
$myTestSuite->printResult();
```

Running the test produces 100% line coverage. However, in the review of test cases that follows, a tester notes that the existing cases still do not adequately test the class. This is due to three changes in code since version 1 of Device:

- The constructor initializes the status with the new value unknown
- set_status() only allows valid status values
- Input validation of status values is now performed by is_validStatus()

The most important new functionality in Device is the new method is_validStatus(), which decides which status values are valid. is_validStatus() has to be tested to ensure that it correctly identifies valid values and rejects invalid ones.

But the current test cases only check the behavior of set_status(). This calls is_validStatus() indirectly but only superficially checks its functionality. The result is that is_validStatus() classifies the status value 'unknown' as invalid. It is not clear how the program should behave, but there are various reasons why is_validStatus('unknown') should return a TRUE value.

Exercise 4.6.2-3 will help you to work through this example.

Is the "every method needs to be tested" rule valid for private methods too?

- **In theory, yes:**
    Otherwise, private methods will only be tested implicitly via calls from public methods—a practice that does not ensure that private methods are adequately tested, even if all test cases return a pass. A private method can contain (defective) code that is not run by the public method that calls it, or it can contain code that only functions correctly in the context of the public method making the call, but in fact

contains defects that only become apparent when the class is reworked or used in a different context by other classes.

Practically speaking, no:

In practice, many testers are happy to test only the API of a class (i.e., its public method and variables)[8]. The problem with this approach is that is makes two potentially critical assumptions:

a) That public methods are tested thoroughly enough so that all indirectly called private methods are automatically tested (thoroughly enough) at the same time.

b) That when a private method is edited, any new defects will be detected by the failure of at least one test case for the public methods.

Even if the test cases for the public methods are thorough, it is not guaranteed (but remains probable) that private methods will be adequately tested. In this case, thorough means:

- Every public method requires test cases defined using equivalence partitioning and boundary value analysis for all the method's parameters.
- The test cases for every private method should be reviewed to check that all equivalence classes and (implicit) boundary values are covered for all parameters[9]. If this is not the case and no additional API test case is drafted, this is an indication of defective design. This could be because a private method has been too generically coded or because it should be transferred to a different (or new) class.

Testing private methods   If you intend to test private methods not just indirectly but also explicitly (along with the APIs), you will confronted with the issue of test cases being unable to call an object's private methods[10]. There are various ways to deal with this issue. You can build the test code into the class you wish to test or you can inject it during the test. However, this approach alters

---

8.   [Meszaros 07, p. 40] calls this the "Use the Front Door First" principle.

9.   100% Line coverage is itself not a sufficient criterion. A private method $p(x)$ could have a parameter x that, for example, is only processed for values of $x<100$. The $x>=100$ branch is either neglected or ignored. If API tests only call this parameter with values <100, this defect will remain undiscovered, even if the resulting line coverage is 100%.

10. This issue can be bypassed in various ways, depending on the programming language you are using. In C++, a test class or test object class can be declared as a friend. PHP uses the setAccessible method in the Reflection API to make private variables accessible.

the production code to make it testable and runs the risk of test code being unintentionally activated in a productive environment, thus causing potentially destructive product behavior. The paradox here is that, while testing is designed to reduce risk, injected test code increases the risk of product malfunction.

Therefore, it is essential to avoid enhancing production code with test code. [Meszaros 07] dedicates two of his 13 principles of good test automation to the concepts of "don't modify the SUT"[11] and "keep test logic out of production code."

Don't modify the SUT.

4.1.3   Object State Testing

The previous section dealt with how to define a sufficient number of meaningful tests for the `public` methods of a class. The test cases thus defined were then used to test each method individually.

Unfortunately, because a class defines variables for its methods, such isolated testing of individual methods is still not sufficient to ensure that a class as a whole will function correctly. At any given moment, every object created by the class thus has a particular state defined by the values assigned to its variables.

The action or reaction of a method thus depends not only on the parameter values used to call it but also on the values assigned to the object's variables. The behavior of an object and its reaction to a particular test case therefore depends on the object's recent history and the state it is in when the test is run. State models are used to define and visualize the desired behavior of an object.

---

11.   SUT = system under test

Case Study 4–3a

eHome Controller 4-3a: State diagram for eHome devices

The eHome team created the following state diagram for the `Device` class:

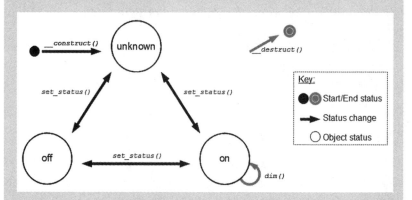

The diagram shows the three possible switching states of a `device` (coded in the `$status`) class variable.

When a `Device` object is created, it initially has the status 'unknown'. This can then be altered using the `set_status` method. The `get_status` method can be called from any status but doesn't alter the status itself. To keep the diagram clear, we have therefore left them out, along with the class variable $name.

Theoretically, the range of values of all of the variables of a class define its state space. In our example, these are the values of the `$status` and $name variables. Because there is no functional interdependency between the two, `Device` has two completely independent state spaces. In the context of the current Sprint, the space determined by $status is the one we are interested in and is the one the team has modeled in the diagram.

State-based testing

An object (or, more generally, a system) whose behavior depends on its recent history is known as state-based, and has to be tested accordingly. The following information is required to fully define a state-based (unit) test case (after [Spillner/Linz 14, section 5.1.3]):

1.   The test object's initial state
2.   The parameter values used to call the method that is to be tested
3.   The expected reaction or return value of the method (including any potential side effects)
4.   The expected successor state of the test object

The state model shows the tester which states the object can be expected to have during its lifetime. The aim of the test is to check whether the object behaves according to its specifications for each of these states. According to [Vigenschow 10], the following aspects of each state need to be tested using appropriate state-based test cases:

- All valid method calls that should be accepted in each state.
- All method calls that are not permissible in each state and which should be rejected.

This approach ensures that every state is tested with positive and negative test cases. Positive cases check that the object functions according to its specifications, while negative ones test whether the object reacts robustly to usage that is contrary to its intended purpose. Defects that are typically revealed using this technique (see [Vigenschow 10, section 9.4.1]) are:

- Missing state transition: A method is rejected even if it should be accepted.
- Non-permissible state transition: A method is accepted although it should be rejected.
- Erroneous action: A method produces an erroneous result.
- Wrong successor state: A method sets the wrong value for a variable, resulting in a non-specified successor state.

---

eHome Controller Case Study 4-3b:
State-based testing of the Device class

Case Study 4–3b

The eHome team reviews the existing test cases to check whether the Device class is already being subjected to state-based testing. They reach the following conclusions:

The test cases for set_status listed in section 4.1.2, "Testing the Methods in a Class," fulfill points 1, 2 and 4 of the definition that states that every set_status test case uses a setup section to set the test object to a particular state, and a check section to check that $status represents the desired resulting state.

The team completely forgot point 3, and the set_status method's (TRUE/FALSE) return values are not checked. Checking the test cases against the state diagram also reveals that there is no test case that switches between the on and off states in either direction. For the user of an eHome system, this is surely the most important use case for a Device object.

Additionally, the test cases neither check whether the entire state space is covered, nor whether states (or method calls) have to be performed in a particular sequence.

4.1.4   State-Based Coverage Criteria

If every state in the model is covered by test cases, the simplest coverage criterion for state-based testing is completely fulfilled. However, as our example illustrates, 100 percent state coverage doesn't mean that all state transitions (i.e., all boundary cases) are triggered and checked. State transition coverage is a stricter criterion[12].

State and state transition coverage

What happens if we use the test strategy described above to check all valid and invalid method calls for each state? In our example, this also guarantees that all transitions are tested. For our sample class, every transition corresponds to a method call (`set_status`). Because all class variables are `private`, there are no states that can be achieved without a method call. Generally however, a tester cannot wholly rely on either of these theories. If a class has `public` variables, direct access to these variables has to be included in the test procedure as if it were a separate class method. And, if the state model describes only the parts of the theoretical state space that are relevant to practical use of the device, there doesn't have to be an obvious direct connection between the method calls of a class and the (application-side) transitions between its states. In such cases, the test strategy described above doesn't cover all transitions.

Path coverage

The third coverage criterion relevant to state-based testing is path coverage, which analyzes which of the available paths through the state model are covered by the existing test cases. As in our eHome example, if transitions between (application) states are associated with specific class methods, appropriate method sequences will create matching paths through the application model. Because state models can exhibit cyclical behavior, paths can be of variable length and of infinite number, even if there is a finite number of boundaries. If you wish to achieve a predefined degree of path coverage, you need to define a maximum possible path length.

---

12. Transition coverage includes state coverage if the state diagram is contiguous (i.e., every state can be reached via at least one transition). A tester has to assume that the product implementation overlooks some transition cases and should always compare the achieved coverage with the (functional) state model.

eHome Controller Case Study 4-3c: Path coverage for the Device class   *Case Study 4–3c*

In our eHome example, we can achieve path coverage of 25% using two paths with a length of four nodes (i.e., two of the eight possible four-node paths):

```
__construct() → set_status('off') → set_status('on') → set_status('unknown');
__construct() → set_status('on') → set_status('off') → set_status('on');
```

The resulting test sequences would include 100% state and boundary case coverage. The illustration below shows the tree diagram for eHome devices:

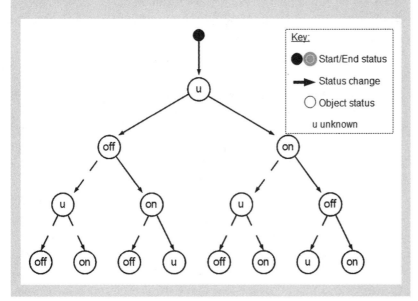

If all negative tests (i.e., those which cover non-permissible method calls) are run in advance or subsequently for all possible states, it is sufficient to build the test sequences themselves from only positive tests. In other words, state coverage alone is enough for the negative tests.

The most effective way to systematically identify all possible paths through a state model is to draw a tree diagram of the model like the one shown above. The relevant procedures are comprehensively described in [Spillner/Linz 14], [Vigenschow 10] and others. The tree diagram can then be used to trace all possible paths up to the predefined maximum length.

Tree diagrams

Any further reduction of the number of test paths should be risk-based and oriented around potential use cases. In many cases, paths mirror the actual usage scenarios of a class and can thus be effectively sorted according to their criticality and frequency of use.

4.1.5 Testing with Method Permutations

The previous section described how to derive test cases from a state model, which offers an abstraction of the program code based on technical reality. For our eHome example we only modeled part of the available state space. The class variable $name was deemed to be technically irrelevant and was not included. The state-based tests we have described are therefore actually specification-based.

So what can you do if you don't have a state model to act as a specification or if a class can only be tested on a code level? [Bashir/Goel 99] describes "method-interaction testing", which works well in such cases, or at least delivers usable heuristics regarding the number and type of tests you should choose.

The jumping-off point is the same as the one described in section 4.1.3, in that the class we wish to test has a number of public methods and private variables. Objects of this class therefore have a specific state and need to be tested using state-based techniques. Because all of its variables are private, the object's state can only be altered using sequences of public method calls.

For example, a class with 10 `public` methods offers a total (S) of 10! (= 3.628.800) call sequences (see [Bashir/Goel 99, section 6.2]), whereby each method is only called once and its parameters are not to be altered.

Slicing a class

The effort involved increases exponentially with the number of methods, but [Bashir/Goel 99] describes a way to drastically reduce the number of concatenated methods. This technique involves slicing a class. Each slice consists of a single class variable and all methods that read from or write to it. A method can appear in multiple slices, whereas a variable can only appear in one and, instead of sequencing methods, only the methods from a single slice are ever combined.

Case Study 4–3d

eHome Controller Case Study 4-3d: Slicing the `Device` class

Version 2 of the Device class offers a total of six call sequences (if we ignore the constructor call):

    S = 3! = 3*2*1 = 6;

`Device` can be sliced into two sub-classes: Sname={get_name()}; Sstatus={set_status(), get_status()}.

The number of required test cases is then:

    S = 1! + 2! = 3;

[Bashir/Goel 99] suggest the following test strategy[13] for a sliced class:

1. Test the constructors and get methods using sequences of the form:
    constructor → reporter[14]

    The reporter reads the appropriate variable value and hands it over to the test class. The test class compares the actual value with pre-defined target values to check that the constructor has initialized the object correctly.

2. Test the get methods using randomly generated sequences of the form:
    constructor → transformer, …, transformer → reporter

    The transformers manipulate the object variables and the reporter has to be capable of delivering a result at the end of each sequence. This is then compared with the contents of the private class variables. The test class needs to be declared as a friend in order to avoid having to manually enter target values for how ever many hundreds or thousands of sequences exist.

3. Test the set methods using randomly generated sequences of the form:
    constructor → transformer, …, transformer

    The transformers manipulate the object variables and thereby the object status, too. Every change of state is followed by a test to see if the correct successor state results. The tester needs to be able to perform local delta checks within each in order to avoid having to manually enter target values for how ever many hundreds or thousands of sequences exist.

If a sequence fails, it is initially unclear which method has caused the failure. To localize the fault, the sequence is shortened step by step until it returns a pass.

This strategy has its shortcomings too, including the necessity to declare the test class as a friend. However, its greatest limitation is that the process doesn't define which parameters are used to call the transformers. In order to ensure that the test nevertheless works when fully automated, we need to use permutations to generate a large number of call sequences. The problem here is that the more sequences we generate, the more difficult it becomes to manually embed call parameters in the test code. Moreover, manually entered parameters cannot be varied.

---

13. We have simplified the description for inclusion here. For full details, see [Bashir/Goel 99].
14. [Bashir/Goel 99] calls get methods reporters and set methods transformers.

What makes this approach interesting (and the reason we mention it here) is that it demonstrates how heuristics can be used to generate call sequences without the use of a functional state model. For cases in which methods require simple (or no) call parameters, it is an elegant way to generate fully automated brute force tests.

4.2 Test First

Section 4.1 introduced some important unit testing basics. The program code (in our example, the class Device) was written and subjected to tests designed using information gleaned from the system's specifications as well as knowledge of the code's structure. These tests were then coded and run automatically. Finally, the programmer had to correct all defects in the code that the tests revealed. Once all this had taken place, the testing procedure began again using the improved code. If this unit testing approach is used consistently within a project (i.e., it is applied to each unit of code and following every alteration), it is an effective way to reveal and remedy shortcomings and errors in the specifications and implementation defects early in the production process.

Before you alter your code, write an automated test that fails.

Test First is an even more effective approach to testing. Like many agile practices, Test First comes from the world of XP. It is one of the most fundamental agile practices and turns the traditional idea of "program first, then test" on its head. Test First means considering which tests will be necessary to show that the software actually fulfills any new specifications before any changes in the code itself are performed. Such tests are designed and automated before they are run. Because the new (or altered) product code doesn't yet exist, the tests will of course fail. Put succinctly, Test First means: Before you alter any code, write an automated test that fails [Beck/Andres 04, p. 50].

The programmer only begins to write the product code once the automated tests exist. If all the tests pass, the coding task is done. If any of the tests fail, the programmer has to work on the code until all tests pass.

Test-driven development

Because the tests drive the developer, we talk about test-driven development, test-first programming, or simply Test First (see also [Link 03]). The frequency with which the programmer applies the "write test → run test → change code" cycle varies from team to team and is also a matter of personal programming style. If a programmer's code is used as part of the team's overall configuration management, this can vary from several times a day (each time the programmer checks his code into the team's configuration management system) right up to continuous unit testing that automatically runs tests for every line of product code as it is written.

A team that uses strict Test First methodology will dramatically increase the effectiveness of its unit testing as a quality management tool. This is because:

Testing replaces trials:
Usually, programmers regularly test the code they are writing to see if it does what it is meant to. If the code requires input, the programmer normally invents appropriate values on the spot. An appropriate parameterized method call is inserted in an appropriate place in the code and target values are only considered vaguely (if at all). Instead of using built-in checks to verify whether a variable has an expected value, the value of the variable in question is usually outputted in the debugger or using a print command. If the program doesn't behave as expected, the programmer tries other input values and the resulting trials end becoming a seamless part of the debugging procedure. This trial and error approach is extremely inefficient. Adding and adjusting new test calls and result output routines takes time and still only reveals the most obvious defects. This approach is equivalent to using a single straight ahead test case and doesn't usually account for special cases, variations or combinations of input values or robustness tests that input invalid data. Conversely, if the programmer takes the time to write a list of meaningful test cases (including input and expected output), effective testing will soon take the place of inefficient, aimless trial and error. The simple act of writing test cases down will help the programmer to think up special cases and interesting combinations of input values. Often, writing it down will help a programmer to find what's missing from the product code without even running the tests themselves. In order to apply the Test First approach effectively, all you have to do is bring writing your test cases forward from "sometime," via "during programming," to "before the first line of code is written."

Test cases provide objective feedback on progress:
If working tests that check the effectiveness of code are available from the start, every passed test the programmer runs provides objective, unequivocal proof that the project has progressed. From the first line of code onward, a programmer can use tests as objective done criteria. This approach reduces the risk of spending hours programming in the

wrong direction and helps to either write new, more relevant tests or to get a failed test to work[15].

Tests replace written specifications:

A test checks whether an object that is fed a particular input value reacts correctly (or returns the correct output). Thus, a test case acts not only as a set of testing instructions but also as the definition of an object's expected behavior. Every test specifies the result that using specific input should produce. Test First thus means specifying a program's behavior in the form of tests before the program is written. Automating these tests thus also creates a precise, machine-readable functional specification for the code that is to be written. In other words, the specifications and the instructions for testing them are one and the same and the separate steps involved in writing both are merged into one. The downside of all this is that less experienced programmers have little chance of properly understanding specifications created this way. This situation can be mitigated by including notes in the test code that explain the rationale behind the test and the input values used. Another way to make tests more human-readable is to write them using an appropriate technical command language, with each command representing a specific function. This type of notation is particularly effective when used for system testing and is explained in more detail in section 6.4.

Test First improves the quality of public interfaces (APIs):

As explained in section 4.1.2, unit tests use the `public` methods of a class to call it. If unit tests are written before the class exists, writing them down defines the names of the `public` methods, the parameters they will have and the use they will be put to. The designs of the test and the API merge into one. The test writer views the test object from the point of view of a future user—in other words, from outside. Because things that are not required to run the test object are not checked by the tests, the tests and test sequences being written will most likely contain only the method calls that future users will need. The result is a clear, lean, application-oriented API.

---

15. "It's clear what to do next: either write another test or make the broken test work"[Beck/Andres 04, p. 51].

■ **Test First improves testability:**

Once the tests have been written, the programmer has to write the code and, where necessary, tweak it until all the tests run faultlessly. This means the code has to include the interfaces required by the tests. Instead of writing test that work with existing code, we now have to write code that is testable using the existing tests. As long as the code isn't completely testable, it isn't finished. If Test First methods are applied strictly (i.e., by every programmer for each change in every unit of code), the resulting effect will filter through to the finest granular level of the code. The resulting code will have appropriate test interfaces at every level of its architecture, all of which can be tested automatically. This makes testing easier and also produces a clearly structured product design that is easier to maintain and extend.

4.2.1   Test First and Scrum

Test First is one of the 13 basic XP practices[16]. Scrum itself doesn't demand the use of Test First and works just as well with traditional unit tests. However, a Scrum Team that uses Test First techniques can benefit significantly on a technical level (see the previous section) and through the acceleration of the feedback loop it provides.

Test First provides each programmer with an additional micro-feed-back loop within each programming task. For every change in the code, the programmer receives immediate feedback about its success or failure. Provided the automated unit tests are efficiently embedded in the team's Continuous Integration process (see chapter 5), the feedback loop can be set to take seconds or minutes.

Micro-feedback loop

Normal unit tests that are written after coding can only check whether changes to the code unintentionally damage existing functionality. They are unable to provide feedback regarding new code that is in the process of being written. The necessary tests don't yet exist and, in the cases of normal unit tests, are only written once the programmer has delivered finished code.

---

16. [Beck/Andres 04] list the following 13 XP Primary Practices: Sit Together, Whole Team, Informative Workspace, Energized Work, Pair Programming, Stories, Weekly Cycle, Quarterly Cycle, Slack, Ten-minute Build, Continuous Integration, Test First Programming, Incremental Design.

In contrast, Test First equips the programmer with all the tests necessary to check new functionality, and the team's unit tests automatically cover the functionality of evolving code.

4.2.2   Implementing Test First

The Test First concept is simple but offers immeasurable benefits. However, using it requires sustained discipline and practice and it still can't be established in a Scrum Team without help.

Change the way you think. It is not at all easy to design and write test cases for test objects that don't exist. To use the idea effectively, programmers and testers have to change the way they think and work. Test First forces you to think in a more abstract way than conventional unit testing, and all the programmers in the team have to learn to think in terms of APIs. Software designers who are used to designing APIs may find it easier to write tests in advance, but those who are used to implementing predefined APIs will find the exercise more difficult. Whatever your skill level, there will always be cases in which writing tests first will turn out to be more difficult than you had hoped, and the temptation to begin coding is hard to resist. The team has to learn to stick rigidly to the Test First concept.

Take account of Test First when planning tasks. This means that Test First has to be actively supported by planning separate test design and automation tasks before planning code implementation tasks. This is the best approach, especially in teams that have little experience of the Test First approach. Once a team has gained some experience, it can begin to use tests as done criteria for feature tasks. It also helps to redesign the task board to follow the "write test → run test → change code" sequence. This way, Test First becomes visible to the whole team and is automatically integrated into the Daily Scrum.

Training and coaching The Scrum Master will also have to support the switch to Test First with additional measures such as training and coaching in the unit testing techniques introduced in section 4.1. Test First doesn't only mean changing the coding/testing sequence, it also commits programmers to the unfamiliar task of writing tests for new functionality and code fragments. This places more stringent demands on the skills required to efficiently perform appropriate tests. Previously, tricky tests could be put aside or left until later, whereas Test First forces you to write tests at every step along the way. But remember: It is of no use to the team if the quality and functionality of these tests is sub-standard. In fact, badly written tests can give a team a false sense of security. The examples listed in section 4.1 illustrate how difficult it can be to write effective tests for even the simplest classes. The power of automated unit tests lies not in the number of tests but rather in the elegance and appropriateness of the test cases themselves, and writing good tests requires solid knowledge of the techniques involved.

The switch to Test First is easier if the team switches to the Pair Programming approach. This requires the team to work in pairs of testers/ programmers. This doesn't mean that the individual roles are always filled by the same person, and they are usually swapped either on a task-for-task basis or at predetermined intervals (for example, every two hours). The people assigned to the pairs themselves can be switched too, and the team is responsible for establishing the rules it uses. The Scrum Master is responsible for initiating the pairing process and needs to intervene if things don't work out. Test code reviews are also an important tool, and should be conducted on a team level and not just within programming pairs, especially while the team is getting used to the new way of working. This will help to stimulate know-how transfer on the subjects of unit test design and automation within the team.

Pair Programming

Test First makes a significant difference in the software development process and the way a team works. Software designers who are used to delivering their own high-blown designs will—at least initially—have problems accepting that other team members have a say in the overall design of the product. Using Test First means that basic design decisions are made on a test-driven basis. Even the most experienced software architect will have to accept that other team members have their own ideas regarding how to create a test-friendly design and may end up altering the test code as a result. Architectural issues—for example, the design of an API or a class, or how external objects should be passed to a class—are now test-driven. Decisions and alternative ideas are viewed much more critically than previously and software design becomes a team effort instead of the result of work done by a single designer or the decisions made by individual programmers. Test First requires, but also accelerates, the transformation of the old team into a cross-functional team. Not every team member will welcome this change, and those who are unable to adapt to it in the long term will have to be replaced.

Test First is a key competence in a Scrum Team and has to be strictly enforced. The Scrum Master is responsible for ensuring that it is introduced and overseen in a suitable fashion.

Test First as a key competence

4.2.3   Using Test First

The eHome team decides to use Test First principles and, as soon as they are identified, all implementation tasks are now given a reference to a corresponding test specification and automation task:

Case Study 4–4a

eHome Controller 4-4a: Test-driven development of the `Dimmer` class

Following the Daily Scrum, one of the programmers pulls a new implementation task from the whiteboard. The team has decided to work according to the principles of Test First and Pair Programming, so the programmer now chooses a tester to work with for the day. The task they have chosen is as follows:

A new class called `Dimmer` is to be derived from the Device class and developed. A dimmer is an electronic actuator that is used to vary the brightness of lamps in a range from 0-100%. A `Dimmer` object represents such a Dimmer actuator within the eHome Controller system.

The done criteria are defined as follows:

- Unit tests automated as `class DimmerTest`
- PHPUnit as test framework
- `class Dimmer` coded
- `DimmerTest` 100% passed with 100% line coverage for `class Dimmer`

Out of habit, the programmer begins to type the first few lines of the new `Dimmer` class, but his partner stops him and reminds him that the `DimmerTest` class has to be created first. They then write the following unit test code together:

```php
include 'Dimmer.php';                    // the class to be tested
include 'TestFrame.php';                 // our simple 'home made'
                                         //   unit test framework
   class DimmerTest extends TestFrame {          // version 1
   public function test_createDimmer() {
                                 // check initial dim-level is 0%
      $dimmer = new Dimmer('lounge chair light');        // setup
      $dimLevel = $dimmer->get_dimLevel();      // test procedure
      $this->assertEquals($dimLevel,0,'createDimmer');   // check
      unset($dimmer);                            // teardown
   }
}

$myTestSuite = new DimmerTest();
$myTestSuite->test_createDimmer();            // execute test case 1
$myTestSuite->printResult();
```

Of course, `test_createDimmer()` doesn't run properly because the test code cannot find the `Dimmer` class[17], which has yet to be programmed. The team has precisely followed the first principles of Test First methodology and created a test that fails as the first step. The test code is simple but nevertheless precisely specifies how the new `Dimmer` class should behave:

- As in the `Device` class, the class constructor is used to set the name of the `Dimmer` object.
- The API method `get_dimLevel()` is used to poll the current brightness setting.
- A newly created `Dimmer` object has a brightness of zero[18].

The corresponding task card defines the planned functionality on a much simpler level. A programmer working without using Test First would have to decide while coding which API methods the class requires and how they should behave. In a Scrum project conducted without Test First, these kinds of design-based decisions wouldn't be explicitly documented, but exist implicitly as part of the source code. In a traditional (e.g., V-model) project environment, these decisions would be made at the specification stage and, if the project is well managed, documented in a fine-grain specification.

In a Test First environment, the test code itself is the specification. Test First therefore not only ensures that the team designs and automates appropriate tests, but also bridges the abstraction gap that otherwise exists between the roughly defined feature task (that belongs conceptually to the system architecture level) and the source code.

The test code is the specification.

Without Test First, the team would have to define a separate "create fine specification" task as a prerequisite for the associated feature task. Test First automatically provides a machine-executable fine specification in the form of automated tests.

---

17. The PHP interpreter issues the message "PHP Fatal error: Class 'Dimmer' not found."
18. The test code uses the Test Frame method `assertEquals()` to check this attribute. See the following chapter for more details.

eHome Controller Case Study 4-4b:
Test-driven development of the `Dimmer` class

The partners discuss the unit test code that they have just written. The tester suggests writing additional test cases, while the programmer would prefer to implement the `Dimmer` class so that the test they have already written passes. There is no reason not to take this approach, and the result is the following code:

```php
include 'Device.php';
class Dimmer extends Device {                           // version 1
private $dimLevel=0;
    public function get_dimLevel() {
    return $this->dimLevel;
    }
}
```

Running the test delivers the following result:

```
Assertions: 1 / passed: 1 / failed: 0
```

Buoyed by this success, the programmer would like to extend the `Dimmer` class, but the tester stops him and reminds him of the agreed rule[a].

They follow the rules and extend the unit test code instead of working on the program code. Instead of their own TestFrame, they also begin to use the unit test framework PHPUnit and re-write their tests accordingly:

```php
include 'Dimmer.php';                      // the class to be tested
class DimmerTest extends PHPUnit_Framework_TestCase {   // version 2
    private $myDimmer;
    public function setUp() {       // setup steps for all test cases
        $this->myDimmer = new Dimmer('lounge chair light');
    }
    public function tearDown() {
        // teardown steps for all test cases unset($this->myDimmer);
    }

    public function test_createDimmer() {
                                    // check, initial dim-level is 0%
        $dimLevel = $this->myDimmer->get_dimLevel();
        $this->assertEquals(0, $dimLevel);
    }
    public function test_set_dimLevel_to_default() {
        $this->myDimmer->set_dimLevel();
        $dimLevel = $this->myDimmer->get_dimLevel();
        $this->assertEquals(50, $dimLevel);  // default shall be 50%
    }
```

```
    public function test_set_dimLevel_to_min() {
        $this->myDimmer->set_dimLevel(0);
        $dimLevel = $this->myDimmer->get_dimLevel();
        $this->assertEquals(0, $dimLevel);        // min shall be 0%
    }
    public function test_set_dimLevel_to_max() {
        $this->myDimmer->set_dimLevel(100);
        $dimLevel = $this->myDimmer->get_dimLevel();
        $this->assertEquals(100, $dimLevel);   // max shall be 100%
    }
    public function test_set_dimLevel_below_min() {
        $this->myDimmer->set_dimLevel(-1);
        $dimLevel = $this->myDimmer->get_dimLevel();
        $this->assertEquals(0, $dimLevel);        // min shall be 0%
    }
    public function test_set_dimLevel_above_max() {
        $this->myDimmer->set_dimLevel(101);
        $dimLevel = $this->myDimmer->get_dimLevel();
        $this->assertEquals(100, $dimLevel);   // max shall be 100%
    }
}
```

They now run the unit tests again, this time called by PHPUnit. However, the test code cannot find the API method set_dimLevel()[b] and halts the test. The missing method can then be easily added to the Dimmer code:

```
    public function set_dimLevel($dimTo=0) {
        if (($dimTo >0) AND ($dimTo <100))
            $this->dimLevel = $dimTo;
    }
```

The unit tests are run once more:

```
> phpunit DimmerTest.v2.php
PHPUnit 3.7.1 by Sebastian Bergmann.
Time: 0 seconds, Memory: 1.50Mb
There were 3 failures:
1) DimmerTest::test_set_dimLevel_to_default
Failed asserting that 0 matches expected 50.
...
2) DimmerTest::test_set_dimLevel_to_max
Failed asserting that 0 matches expected 100.
...
3) DimmerTest::test_set_dimLevel_above_max
Failed asserting that 0 matches expected 100.
...
Tests: 6, Assertions: 6, Failures: 3.
```

> The programmer was adamant that he had written this trivial method correctly, but corrects the code while secretly admitting that Test First is not such a bad idea after all.

    a. "Write a failing automated test before changing any code" [Beck/Andres 04, S. 50].
    b. `PHP Fatal error: Call to undefined method Dimmer::set_dimLevel()`

You can perform the correction yourself in exercise 4.6.3-1 or check out the correct version at our website [URL: SWT-knowledge].

4.3 Unit Testing Frameworks

Automating a unit test is basically quite simple. The examples we have used so far follow the following pattern:

- For the class `'xyz'` that is to be tested (the test object), we have to create a test class `'xyzTest'` (the test driver).
- The test cases are automated as methods of the test class `'xyzTest'`. Each test case is implemented by one unique method.
- Test method names are chosen to reflect the content of the corresponding test case. This helps to make the unit tests easy to identify and maintain.
- Each test case (or test case method) is divided into four sections called `'setup'`, `'test procedure'`, `'check'` and `'teardown'`. Each test is designed to check only a single aspect of the test object, which in turn means that a test method should only ever contain one `'check'` section.
- A `'check'` compares the actual with the expected outcomes. In other words, it checks whether the state of a particular object attribute (defined by one or more class variables) agrees with the desired (specified) value.
- If the expected and actual values agree the test is `'passed'`. If they differ, the test is `'failed'`.
- Test cases can be started either individually using the corresponding methods or as a batch using the `'run'` method provided by the test framework. This usually takes place in the sequence they appear in the class.

All test cases and test classes are programmed the same way; therefore, the result is a large number of similar lines of code. Recurring steps are coded in a separate framework class. The examples up to 4-4a use a simple test framework class `TestFrame`, which provides the central check function `assertEquals` that also collects the individual test results. It also provides the function `printResult` for outputting the results. All test classes inherit these functions (see example 4-4a: `DeviceTest extends TestFrame`).

`TestFrame` can be further extended to include functions that record dated test results or import test data from a table. The framework should also be capable of recognizing which test cases a test class contains, and should be able to run them as a batch without the tester having to call each using a separate line of code. It is also helpful to include identical `setUp` and `teardown` steps in the framework whence they can be automatically activated before and after each test case.

If you are involved in automating unit tests, you can add such additional functionality using pre-coded unit test frameworks. These are produced as open source projects and are available free of charge on the Web for most popular programming languages. The Java version is called JUnit, the C++ version CppUnit, and NUnit for .Net. All three are based on the SUnit framework designed and introduced by Kent Beck in 1998 (see [URL: SUnit]) and, as a result, have similar structures. This similarity gives rise to the widely used term "xUnit frameworks"[19].

xUnit frameworks

In our eHome case study, we use the PHPUnit framework [URL: PHPUnit]. If you compare the test code in figures 4-2 and 4-4, you will see how using a framework can simplify the structure of the test code.

4.4   Stubs, Mocks and Dummies

The versions of the class `Device` that we have shown you so far have no dependencies on other components of the eHome system. The class is executable and can thus be tested independently using unit tests. However, in practice, unit tests are usually performed on objects that are components of a larger system, and are dependent on other components, without which they cannot run.

Therefore, to test an object, all dependent components have to be installed in the test environment. The problem here is that the Test First approach is designed to avoid exactly this type of situation by testing each object individually. Additionally, if they are due to be implemented in later Sprints, some or all of the additional components may not be available at testing time.

---

19. [Meszaros 07] describes xUnit frameworks in detail.

The solution to this quandary is to replace any depended-on components (DOCs) with placeholders known as test doubles. [Meszaros 07] defines the following types of doubles:

Fig. 4–1

Types of placeholders

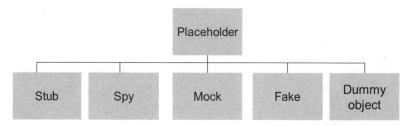

■ **Stub:**
Replaces a DOC with a component that has an identical interface that produces specific reactions or returns certain values according to a predefined pattern. From the point of view of the test, a stub acts as an additional indirect input parameter.

■ **Spy:**
A stub that includes an additional mechanism that records calls and data handed over by the test object. The recorded data can then be used to back up the test results or help with diagnosis and debugging.

■ **Mock:**
A "smart" stub that analyzes calls and data that it receives from the test object for validity, and also independently returns a reaction or result to the object. From the point of view of the test, a mock acts as an additional verification step for the test object's `indirect output`.

■ **Fake:**
Uses highly simplified implementation to replace a DOC that is required for testing but which has no influence on the test results.

■ **Dummy:**
A "pseudo-object," "empty object," or "null pointer" that replaces a data object required syntactically by the test object. A dummy is not interpreted and therefore forms no part of the test data.

When estimating effort, a Scrum Team should be aware that such placeholders play a more significant role than they do in traditionally managed projects:

■ Incremental development usually means that some of the required components are either not ready or don't yet exist. To prevent a unit test from being blocked and to ensure the flow of relevant feedback, it is essential to use placeholders to replace missing components.

▨ Test First automatically runs existing unit tests every time the corresponding code is altered. This can happen multiple times within the space of just minutes, so it is important that the duration of each test run is kept to a minimum. This necessity is another good reason to use stubs, mocks and other placeholders.

Coding the required placeholders is part of the test automation process and can involve a significant amount of effort. This has to be accounted for when planning a Sprint.

4.5   Unit Test Management

Test management is often neglected, regardless of whether a team is working in a traditional or an agile project. It is often simply assumed that traditional developers or a Scrum Team will somehow automatically perform the required unit tests without the use of specific instructions or agreements. In reality, there are a number of aspects of the test management process that need to be agreed upon:

▨ **Unit test framework:**
The Scrum Master (or Test manager[20]) has to make sure that all team members write similarly structured tests. It is essential to avoid situations in which each programmer manages their own unit tests on a separate development machine and the team doesn't know which tests exist, where they can be found, or when (or if) they have been run. Tests have to be stored centrally on the team's development network in a file system with an agreed structure. To keep installation (or, as the case may be, delivery) simple, it is advisable to store test code separately from program code using parallel folders[21]. You also need to establish naming rules for test classes and cases as well as for the structure of each test case (see section 4.1.2). A test manager should urge the team to use a predefined xUnit framework and proprietary frameworks should only be used in exceptional cases. It is definitely more produc-

---

20. Section 3.7.2 explains how this role is filled within a Scrum Team.
21. In order to better illustrate the interplay between program and test code, our case study stores both in the same directory.

tive if the team invests its time and energy in the design and automation of tests rather than in the creation of a bespoke framework.

Coverage measurement:
The Scrum Master (or test manager) has to ensure that test coverage is measured reliably and its Sprint-by-Sprint development analyzed regularly. This requires the integration of a suitable coverage measurement tool in the CI environment (see chapter 5). This should at least be able to measure and output class coverage, method coverage per class and the line or statement coverage within each method. Of course, such measurements only make sense if the team agrees in advance on appropriate coverage limits. Even in a Scrum project, it is impossible to test all parts of a program's code equally thoroughly and coverage limits can differ from subsystem to subsystem and from unit to unit. The necessary coverage limits should be established in accordance with the risk analysis performed for each unit.

Static code analysis:
Dynamic unit tests should be supplemented by appropriate static code analysis. The best tool to use will depend on the programming language being used and, once selected, the tool needs to be parameterized and integrated into the CI environment (see chapter 5). Ultimately, the code analysis tool should automatically check that the team sticks to all of its self-imposed rules. Any coding rules that the team uses (or is planning to use) that cannot be checked automatically should be discarded.

Program code reviews:
The Scrum Master (or test manager) should ensure that regular program code reviews take place[22]. A program code review should question whether the current class hierarchy adequately represents the planned system architecture, whether the APIs are appropriate to the classes and whether code restructuring could improve code quality and maintainability. The clean code patterns described in [Martin 08][23]

---

22. In this context, the term "review" is an umbrella term that refers to inspection, walkthrough, pair review and other review practices. The most appropriate review type will depend on the risk assessment for each unit.

23. These include recipes for naming identifiers and variables, naming and structuring classes and class methods, formatting and commenting source code, and tips on naming and structuring automated tests.

provide a wealth of useful tips and tricks for recognizing when restructuring is appropriate.

Test code reviews:
Test code should be reviewed regularly too. The main reason for doing so is to check what a test is designed to do and how effectively it performs its allotted task. Reviews serve to check whether the team is using appropriate test design techniques, such as equivalence partitioning, boundary value analysis or state-based testing. If this analysis reveals any deficiencies, the team should consider initiating appropriate training. A review will also help to reveal which test cases still need to be written to cover all the specifications of a feature or class.

Every Scrum Team should have targets and agreements for the points listed above. If these don't yet exist, the Scrum Master needs to take the initiative and get the team to get organized and elect a test manager. All agreements reached are documented in the Team Charter (see section 3.6). Like all commitments made during a Scrum project, these too can and should be modified from Sprint to Sprint as the team continues to learn. This is the approach taken by the eHome team:

The Team Charter documents the team's rules.

---

eHome Controller Case Study 4-5: Extending the Team Charter

Case Study 4–5

During the retrospective following the first Sprint, the team discusses the state of its unit testing efforts. They conclude that they are doing fine and, to ensure that things stay this way, the Scrum Master agrees with the team to add the following unit test guidelines to the Charter:

> **Team Charter**
> – How we aim to apply Scrum to the eHome Controller project –
> ...
> Practices
>   ...
>   Unit testing:
>   – Test First! Write a test that fails before altering any code
>   – Every class has its own test class
>   – There is at least one test case for every `public` method
>   – Every test class is reviewed by a second team member

The most experienced tester in the team is given the role of test manager and is now responsible for overseeing all testing tasks—a move that helps to relieve some of the pressure on the Scrum Master, who only supports the team part-time.

4.5.1   Unit Test Planning

The main thrust of unit testing is to check the functionality and robustness of a software unit when it is subjected to inappropriate use (for example, if it is called using invalid parameters), and it is the test manager's job to ensure that unit testing remains focused on these two factors. We have already introduced and described suitable test design methods at the beginning of this chapter.

Plan placeholder programming

Unit tests are designed to test the test object in isolation from other program components and the unit test suite should perform these tests as quickly as possible. To effectively fulfill both these criteria, it is essential to use placeholders (see Stub above). Programming placeholders is part of the test automation process and can involve a lot of effort, which in turn has to be accounted for when planning a Sprint. A Scrum Team's test manager has to make sure that placeholders do actually get programmed. If this task is forgotten or ignored (perhaps to save time), the associated unit test will be impossible to perform until all the components that interact with the test object have been completed, thus significantly increasing the time it takes to perform unit testing.

Add non-functional unit tests

Once a number of Sprints have produced a sufficient number of high-quality automated tests, you can extend the unit test suite to include non-functional tests—for example, to check performance attributes at class level. Such non-functional tests do not, however, guarantee non-functional aspects of the finished product, which have to be checked using non-functional tests at a system level. On the other hand, they do help to identify existing weaknesses at an early stage, so it does help to use unit tests to check the non-functional aspects of units whose purpose or position within the system architecture influences the overall behavior of the product. This approach helps to realize the potential for early recognition of performance issues that would otherwise only become apparent during system testing.

4.6   Questions and Exercises

4.6.1   Self-Assessment

Questions and exercises to help you assess how agile your project or team really is.

1. Has the team already written automated unit tests? How many? For which classes?
2. Do our programmers manage their own tests or are all unit tests managed centrally? Are we using a unit test framework?
3. In which environment are the tests performed? On the programmer's own machine or on a CI server? Is the test environment adequately defined and is it reproducible?
4. When are unit tests performed? Is this decision up to the programmer? During build runs? When code is checked into the configuration management system? Automatically within the Continuous Integration environment (see section 5.5)?
5. Which coverage criteria do we use? Class coverage (i.e., each class requires its own test class)? Method coverage (i.e., at least one test case per `public` method)? Line coverage? Branch coverage? Path coverage? State-based coverage?
6. Which target coverage values do we use? How often are these values measured? Which coverage values do we actually achieve?
7. Which values have we achieved now/today? Where does the team store these values? Where can they be found if I want to know them now?
8. Do we perform test case reviews? Regularly? What conclusions do we come to? Which measures have been introduced to improve test coverage and/or the quality of our unit tests?
9. Which test design techniques do we use? Equivalence partitioning? Boundary value analysis? State-based testing? Has the team been trained to use these techniques?
10. When are tests designed? Before coding begins (Test First)? After executable code for the unit has been written? At the end of the Sprint?
11. Who analyzes the test results and logs and checks whether a feature is done?

12. Which rules do we use to decide which defects are to be managed using the defect management system? How do we ensure that all defects are addressed and corrected?

13. In addition to unit testing, which quality assurance measures does the team use? Automated code analysis? Code reviews?

14. Are quality assurance and testing (and the results thereof) discussed in the Daily Scrum and the retrospectives? What new conclusions have we drawn? Which specific improvement actions have we agreed on? Which of these is currently being implemented?

4.6.2   Methods and Techniques

These questions will help you to review the content of the current chapter.

1. Which sections make up a unit test (case)? Explain the purpose of each.

2. What is the line coverage result of running `test_KitchenLightOn` for version 2 of the class `Device` shown in case study 4-2a?

3. Add a test case `test_setStatusUnknown` that checks whether the status value `unknown` is classified as *valid* by `is_validStatus()`. Why is this additional testing step necessary here and not in the other cases for this class?

4. Take a look at the state diagram in case study 4-3a. If the unit tests for the class achieve 100% line coverage on a code level, are all class methods called at least once? Can we safely conclude that the tests in the state model achieve 100% boundary coverage? If yes, why?

5. Explain why using Test First produces better APIs and better overall testability.

6. Which problems can occur when introducing Test First and how can a Scrum Master counteract them?

4.6.3   Other Exercises

These exercises will help you delve deeper into topics touched on in the course of the chapter.

1. Edit the method `set_dimLevel()` from the `Dimmer` class so that the test cases listed in case study 4-4b run successfully.

2. Use the methods described by [Bashir/Goel 99] to slice the Dimmer class. Which slices result? Which test case sequences then need to be run for Dimmer?

3. The action dim('0%') is meant to switch a device to its 'off' state. Draft a test case that specifies this behavior.

4. The dim command should have no effect on a device in the states unknown and off. Draft test cases that specify this behavior.

5. The code of the Dimmer class is extended to encompass these new requirements, resulting in a new version 3. Does this version contain slices other than those you have already listed? If yes, what effect does this have on the required test sequences?

6. The eHome system is to be extended to include timed switching commands with the help of a new class called Timer. Because the team uses Test First, it has to draft appropriate test cases for the new class. Draft the unit test cases required to specifiy the following behavior for the Timer class:

    set_interval() specifies the number of seconds the timer runs for. start() starts the timer, and stop() stops it. is_finished()[24] returns TRUE when the set time runs out and FALSE otherwise.

    Which loopholes can you identify in these specifications?

---

24. For the purposes of this exercise, we will ignore the fact that a real timer would have to trigger an interrupt or an interrupt handler.

5   Integration Testing and Continuous Integration

This chapter explains the differences between unit and integration testing, how to design integration test cases and how to embed them in a fully auto-mated Continuous Integration (CI) environment along with the unit tests we have already written.

5.1   Integration Testing

A software system is made up of multiple components. For the system to work properly, each component has to function reliably on its own and, most importantly, all the components have to work together as planned. Integration testing checks whether this is the case.

Integration tests are designed to discover potential defects in the inter-action of the individual components and their interfaces. In order to per-form an integration test, two components are connected (i.e., integrated) and activated by appropriate integration test cases. Fig. 5-1 shows a sche-matic example of an integration test involving two classes.

Integration tests check the interaction of the individual components.

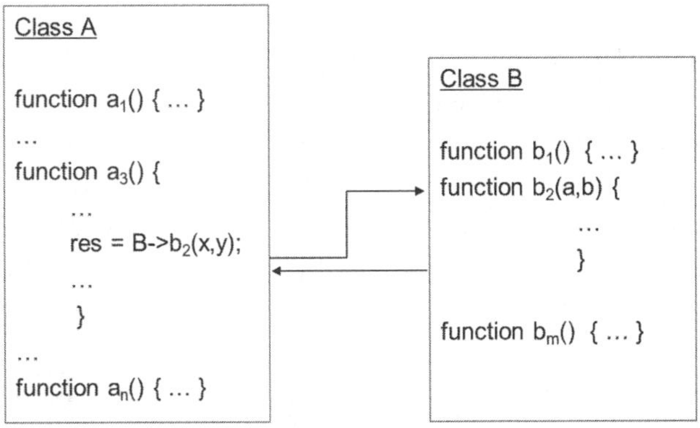

Fig. 5–1

An integration test involving two classes

The interface of Class A is comprised of methods a_1, a_2, ..., a_n, while Class B comprises the methods b_1, b_2, ..., b_m. Both classes have passed all their corresponding unit tests. The integration tests that we will now define test whether A and B work together properly. In our example, the interaction takes place between method b_2 and its call from method a_3[1]. We thus need to check whether b_2 is called correctly and whether it then returns the desired result to A.

5.1.1   Typical Integration Failures and Their Causes

Although A and B function correctly on their own, there are various defective behaviors that can turn up when they work in concert. The most important of these are interface failures:

- A calls the wrong method from B:
  If we assume that A is a class within the eHome Controller's user interface and B is the class that represents individual devices, to switch off the kitchen lamp A would have to call the method `switch('kitchen', 'lamp', 'off')` in B. However, A has been wrongly coded `dim('kitchen', 'lamp', '50')`.
- A calls the correct method from B, using invalid parameter values:
  As an example, A is meant to switch on the kitchen lamp but calls `switch('living_room', 'lamp')` instead. The first parameter is semantically incorrect, while the third parameter is missing entirely.
- The paired components code the returned data differently:
  In A, the call `dim('kitchen', 'lamp', '50')` means that the lamp is dimmed to 50% brightness using a value coded with values between 0 and 100. However, the `dim()` method in B expects the brightness value to be coded as a floating-point number between 0 and 1 (in this case, 0.5).
- A calls the desired method correctly but at the wrong time or in the wrong sequence (see section 4.1.3).
  As an example, the required object in B doesn't yet exist at the moment A accesses B and causes a runtime error in A. Even if the object in B already exists, it could be that one of its variables has either not been initialized or has been initialized with an incorrect value. This results either in a runtime error in B or, because of the erroneous variable, in B

---

1.   Class A requires an object from class B to make it executable. In other words, A is dependent on B.

returning an incorrect value to A. Once A begins to work with an incorrect value, further failures are inevitable.

If the components communicate asynchronously[2], The following additional failures can also occur:

Timing failures

- A hands over data when B is not ready to receive it.
- B returns a result to A either too early or too late. A cannot receive or process the returned data.
- A fails to recognize the timeout or reacts wrongly to it (for example, by repeating the call).

Throughput or capacity failures

- A hands over more data than B can handle within a specific period of time, resulting in lost data or data overflow in B.
- B returns more data than A can process.

Performance problems

- A hands over data faster or more often than B can handle and ends up waiting or re-sending data. The result is that processing speed between the two components decreases to below the specified minimum.

If the two components are distributed across separate hardware systems, **transmission failures** can also occur:

- The connection (the local network, for example) is damaged or down, resulting in the transmission of false, garbled, or no data.

If the components concerned were developed by different programmers or teams, the risk of integration defects increases. In such cases, the root cause of the defect is usually misunderstanding or differing interpretation of the specification or a simple lack of communication between the responsible developers.

Causes of failures

Changes to code and software updates can also cause defects—for example, if one component is altered but another that depends on it isn't.

---

2.   Unlike in a synchronous communications loop in which the components involved wait for a response from the other side before sending or receiving data, the components in an asynchronous loop send and receive data without waiting for a response, reading and writing data to and from a shared data buffer.

The compilers in compiler-based and statically typed programming languages usually detect these types of syntactical interface defects, whereas many interpreter-based languages (PHP, for example) only detect such defects at runtime.

> **eHome Controller Case Study 5-1:**
> **Integration defects due to incomplete refactoring**
>
> The method `set_status()` in the `Device` class has been extended to include the `write()` call that writes an appropriate string to the data-base buffer when a valid change in status takes place. However, the person programming the database interface has renamed the class `writeMsg()` but forgotten to rename the method call in the Device class accordingly. Because the programmer has switched off the PHP interpreter's error messages, this defect initially remains undiscovered and only comes to light during the nightly integration test run when the `write()` call causes a runtime error.

Due to the continual alteration and improvement of the code that agile processes involve, the risk of code changes or updates causing integration defects is particularly prevalent in an agile environment. Therefore, even if just a single component is altered, you should always re-run not only its unit test but also all the integration tests that cover components that it interacts with.

5.1.2   Designing Integration Test Cases

Integration test cases are designed to detect defects of the types listed above. If components A and B are integrated in such a way that A uses B, A requires test cases that trigger all relevant usages of B. The corresponding test setup then looks like this:

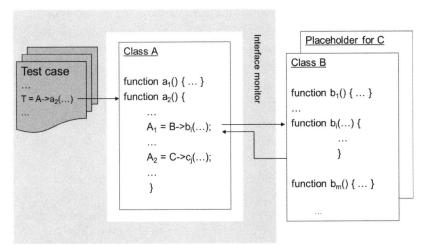

Fig. 5–2

*Integration test setup
and interfaces*

To systematically derive the required integration test cases, follow these steps:

*Systematically deriving
integration test cases*

1. Analyze interaction: Identify and list which services and methods in B are used by A. Identify—for example, using the architecture diagram—whether interactions with other components exist and, if they do, set appropriate placeholders in the test environment.

2. Equivalence partitioning: For each identified service or method, analyze which sets of parameters and/or messages are handed over and use equivalence partitioning to identify which of these are relevant to the behavior of the affected components.

3. Establish test case input: Identify the calls or call sequences in A's API that are necessary to call B using the parameter sets and messages identified in step 2 above, thus covering all the identified equivalences.

4. Define an expected/actual comparison: Define expected behavior for A and B for each test input case and establish where and how the expected reaction can be analyzed. This will be either the APIs of A and/or B, the indirect output from A and/or B, or logged data traffic that is handled by the transmitting interface.

5. Test robustness of asynchronous communication: For asynchronous calls for B, we require additional tests that check for and remedy timing, throughput, capacity, and performance defects. Components that are distributed between multiple hardware environments also need to be tested to ensure that the data transfer between them is stable and reliable.

Step 5 is only necessary if the components in question run parallel and are connected asynchronously. If this is the case, robustness tests that deliberately provoke critical situations (e.g., a timeout) are essential to establish whether the integrated system has sufficient failure tolerance built in.

This approach can also be used to test compound components made up of multiple units—in other words, to design integration test cases for complex subsystems or for overall system integration testing (see section 5.3).

Case Study 5–2

eHome Controller Case Study 5-2: Robust reaction when the connection is interrupted

An eHome Controller `Device` object can only change its switching state (e.g., from on to off) once the device in question has either physically or virtually performed the switching action and has returned an acknowledge message. If this confirmation arrives within the predefined timeout limit, the `Device` object will switch its state. If the confirmation doesn't arrive on time, the `Device` object will repeat the switching operation.

The eHome system architecture (see fig. 3-2 on page 31) gives rise to three places where the connection between the eHome Controller and the device can be interrupted:

a) eHome Controller ↔ Message buffer (database)
b) Message buffer (database) ↔ Bus adapter
c) Bus adapter ↔ Bus system

The integration test needs to check that the eHome Controller reacts correctly without having to connect the system to a real, physical bus the way it is during system testing.

The following simulation is used to test situation a):
Once it has sent the switching message, the test shuts the connection to the database. In this state, the message should *not* be repeated, as it can already be relayed onward. Instead, once the database connection has been re-established, a recovery run is triggered that once again polls the status of all attached devices and imports the results to the database. However, this functionality is scheduled for implementation in a later Sprint.

To test situation b), the test setup empties the message buffer to ensure that no messages can be exported. The timeout limit is set to a minimal value to make sure that the integration test isn't slowed down unnecessarily. To test whether the `Device` object has repeated its switching message, the test checks whether the database now contains two identical switching messages.

To test situation c), the bus adapter is replaced by a stub that can be parameterized and that sends (or doesn't send) an acknowledge message once the timeout limit has been reached following each switch command.

5.1.3 The Differences between Unit and Integration Tests

For a programmer, integration tests are very similar to unit tests. Both types of test cases access the test object via its API and, in most projects, use the same framework for test automation (the eHome team uses the PHPUnit framework for both). Because of these technical similarities, unit and integration tests are often not clearly distinguished, even though they are used to test very different attributes of the software under test:

- **Unit test cases** are designed to check whether individual software components (e.g., a single class and its methods) work correctly. The test checks the internal functionality of the unit and its robustness when it is confronted with misuse (e.g., a call that uses invalid parameters). The test cases have to cover the unit's methods and their parameters as far as possible. The component in question is tested in isolation and other components required to run the test are represented by placeholders. This approach means that any defects that are discovered are caused by defects within the component being tested.

- **Integration test cases** are designed to check whether two interdependent software components (e.g., two classes) work correctly in concert. The test analyzes and checks as many different variations of the data transfer between the components as possible. The components are connected during the test, and any defects that are discovered can be clearly attributed to one or the other of the two or, in the case of distributed components, to the communication channel.

- **Test coverage:** For the setup shown above, if the unit tests for component A are run, it is possible that this will coincidentally trigger interaction between A and B that is covered by the existing integration tests. By the same token, if the unit tests for B are run too, this won't necessarily produce coverage that accurately mirrors the intended coverage of the integration tests. Conversely, if integration tests are used as unit tests, these are highly likely to include redundant tests for methods belonging to A that are triggered by interaction between the two components, and will most probably also show gaps in the testing of methods that require no interaction.

- **Testing tools:** In addition to the frameworks used by unit and integration tests, integration tests also use monitors to diagnose and output (in human-readable form) the data traffic that passes through the interfaces, buses and networks that belong to the test environment. Monitoring tools for common protocols such as TCP/IP are freely available and are built into some operating systems (for example, the Linux "tcpdump" command). To monitor project-specific interfaces and protocols, teams will either have to develop bespoke monitoring tools or redesign existing ones.

When software components are integrated, it is not sufficient to simply repeat each unit's unit tests to check the interaction between them. Interaction between components nearly always produces new situations that have to be covered by additional specific integration tests. In spite of their technical similarities, it is important to differentiate clearly between the two types of tests and to develop each test suite using the test design guidelines detailed here and in chapter 4.

5.2   The Role Played by System Architecture

Chapter 4 introduced some basic rules of thumb covering the minimum number of unit tests required to test a class. The following sections investigate the possibility of using similar rules to estimate the effort involved in integration testing.

Our intuition tells us that the larger and more complex a system is, the greater the number of integration tests we will need to test it thoroughly. To simplify things, the size of a system can be expressed in terms of the number of components that needs to be integrated, while its complexity can be expressed using the number of dependencies that exist between them. The subsystem shown in fig. 5-1 consists of two classes (A and B), whereby A is dependent on B. Using the notation described above, this gives us a system of size 2 and a complexity of 1.

Because each component can also be dependent on other parts of the system, the number of dependencies is often disproportionate to the number of components and can even grow exponentially. The development of these proportions depends on the architecture of the system being tested, as illustrated in fig. 5-3.

Figure 5-3 shows the growth in the number of dependencies (k) in relation to the number of components in a system. If the components are connected using a tree structure, this growth is linear and can be expressed using the formula $k=(n-1)$, whereas networked connections result in quadratic growth expressed by $k=n(n-1)/2$.

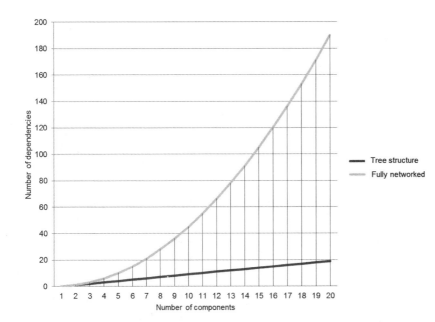

When counting dependencies, every direction has to be counted sepa-rately. If components A and B communicate bilaterally, both dependencies (A-to-B and B-to-A) have to be tested. Detailed discussions on the subjects of interfaces, dependencies, and their effects on integration testing can be found in [Winter et al. 12].

---

eHome Controller Case Study 5-3: Dependencies between the controller component and the bus device

Case Study 5–3

Clicking the browser-based button "Kitchen lamp on" triggers the message `switch( 'kitchen', 'lamp', 'on')` and sends it to the bus. The electronic switch that is used to switch the lamp on has to act on this message and confirm the action with the acknowledge message "lamp is on."

The corresponding integration test has to cover two cases:

- Send `switch( 'kitchen', 'lamp', 'on')` and check that the switch (the actuator) performs the required action
- Check in the browser if the acknowledge message arrives within the prescribed timeout period

In this case, two test steps are necessary because two separate depen-dencies exist between the browser and the switch.

5.2.1   Dependencies and Interfaces

Counting the dependencies in a system is more difficult than estimating its size (for example, by counting the number of classes it contains). Such dependencies are not always explicit and are often implied by indirect connections within the system:

- An explicit dependency exists if (as shown in fig. 5-1) a component A calls a component B directly via its API. The fact that A is dependent on component B is obvious from reading the code. Explicit dependencies can therefore be identified either by the compiler or using static code analysis (i.e., without actually running the components concerned).
- An implicit (i.e., indirect) dependency exists if multiple components share a single resource. For example, if two or more components access the same global variable, use the same file or access the same database.

Indirect dependency via shared resources

Indirect dependency is caused by the twin facts that component A writes to the shared resource (thus altering the content of the data object) while the behavior of component B (or others) varies depending on that same content. Although the two components don't explicitly call each other, read components are indirectly influenced by the actions of any components that write to the shared data object. Additionally, if two components read from and write to a shared object, a bilateral interaction develops. However, the code itself reveals only that each component accesses that particular resource—not whether or when other components use it too.

Indirect dependencies are all too easy to overlook and the corresponding components are therefore often left out when it comes to integration testing. However, if these dependencies are identified in time, the tests they require can be defined the same way as those used to test explicitly dependent objects:

- Integration tests for explicitly dependent components have to cover all relevant variations on their method calls (i.e., all relevant combinations of parameters) or, in the case of asynchronous communication, the transfer of data between components.
- For indirectly dependent components, integration tests either have to cover all relevant combinations of read/write sequences that affect the shared resource and/or the relevant possible contents of the shared resource. The latter can require the creation or provision of large amounts of test data.

5.2.2   Testability and Testing Effort

While the number of unit tests depends on the number of components[3], the required number of integration tests depends on the number of dependencies that exist between them. The number of dependencies depends on the nature of the system architecture.

Modern systems built using object-oriented design and programming techniques tend to have strongly cross-linked architectures made up of a large number of small, interacting classes. This type of structure makes integration testing more significant than it is for other system architectures. [Winter et al. 12] states that "… object-oriented methods have shifted the major sources of defects from modules (or classes) to the interactions between classes. Most defects and nearly all critical defects in an object-oriented system can [therefore] only be discovered through integration testing."

Integration testing can involve a lot of effort, especially when a cross-linked system architecture contains a disproportionate number of dependencies compared with the number of components that produces them. Conversely, the effort involved in integration testing can be significantly reduced if the overall system architecture is suitably simplified.

In addition to object-oriented techniques, the iterative nature of Scrum projects also increases the required testing effort. If a Sprint adds new features to the system, this usually involves the addition of new classes or other software components. This means not only that the existing integration tests have to be repeated for every iteration, but also that new tests have to be designed, automated and performed.

To prevent the integration testing effort from increasing too quickly, it is essential to keep an eye on the system architecture and to perform regular refactoring to keep it simple.

The effort involved in integration testing also depends on the testability of the individual interfaces. According to [Spillner/Linz 14], testability describes the ease and speed with which the functionality and performance of a system can be (regularly) tested. A poorly testable system requires more effort to test than an easily testable one.

Integration testing effort and testability

With regard to the dependencies and interfaces that integration testing is designed to check, easily testable dependencies are simple to identify within the source code, are easy to access via the test framework, and are

---

3.   This is a simplified assessment that assumes that all classes have a similar number of methods with a similar number of internal interactions.

easy to observe (for example, using a documented API call or an interface monitor). An interface is also easy to test if it is "lean" (i.e., the number of data variations that have to be covered is small). The effort involved in integration testing therefore relates directly to the number of dependencies involved and their individual testability.

These are both attributes of the system architecture, so a good architecture will be made up of easily distinguishable subsystems that interact via a small number of explicit, lean interfaces.

System architecture can be improved by transforming implicit dependencies into explicit ones—for instance, by encapsulating shared global resources in separate classes that then provide access to the resource by way of an API-based service. This makes API calls simple to identify within the code, and it means that identification and handling of invalid data can take place centrally. In turn, this means that the required tests don't have to be performed for each individual component that uses the resource. Additionally, the complexity of the components using the service is reduced and the robustness testing effort is transferred from the integration tests for the components that use the service to the unit tests that cover the service class.

5.3 Integration Levels

The preceding sections describe how to develop integration tests for individual classes. Repeated integration necessarily combines elemental components in packages and subsystems that can then be treated as independent components in their own right. Components that are to be integrated show differing levels of granularity depending on the level of abstraction on which the integration process takes place.

5.3.1 Class Integration

The integration of classes is the lowest level on which integration testing takes place. In the world of object-oriented programming, smaller units (individual methods, for example) are encapsulated within a class and are tested as part of a unit test. However, when integrating classes[4], various integration types can be clearly identified:

---

4. [Vigenschow 10] and [Winter et al. 12] include comprehensive discussions of suitable test sequences and the challenges presented by inheritance issues.

■ **Vertical integration** describes classes that are integrated along the lines of their inheritance hierarchies. If class B inherits its attributes from class A, all non-private methods and variables in A will be available to B and can be called in or used by B. If class A is altered (for example, if the implementation of a feature is changed during a Sprint), it is likely that A's methods will act differently as a result. This also means that calls of A from B can fail or behave differently. Therefore, an integration test of the interaction between A and B has to be repeated after every change in A. Methods in B (e.g., m_B) can also overwrite methods that belong to A (e.g., m_A), so changes in B have to be followed by repeat tests too. As an example, if the name of m_B: is altered (perhaps unintentionally), m_A will be called instead of m_B, which can lead to completely different program behavior. Such tests can be seen as integration tests between objects that belong to a single inheritance hierarchy. However, in most cases, only a single runtime object will exist that runs the code in its methods (the fact that some of this code was inherited makes no difference to the object). Viewed this way, tests that follow an inheritance hierarchy can also be viewed as unit tests. The way a Scrum Team handles such tests is of secondary importance to the necessity of having appropriate inheritance tests available for re-use following changes in the code.

■ **Horizontal integration** describes class association relations between two classes with no inherited attributes and with at least one object of each existing at runtime—i.e., one class uses the other. If A calls a method from B, a dependency exists that has to be appropriately integration tested.

■ **Compound classes and objects:** A special kind of "A uses B" dependency exists if class A contains class B in the form of a data structure. If A accesses B, it uses the methods and/or variables in B. In such cases, an explicit integration test between A and B is often overlooked because B is seen as being part of A. Unit testing A tests B implicitly but only coincidentally. If the code has been cleanly written, drafting an explicit test is tricky, as B is encapsulated by A and is thus private. This makes it difficult to observe B's behavior during a test. One work-around is to use Dependency Injection (see [Meszaros 07, chapter 26] for examples), which doesn't embed the dependent object (in our case class B) as a variable of A, but instead hands it over to A's constructor as a parameter, making it visible from outside. Using this approach, B can be replaced by a spy for integration testing, or by a stub or a mock for unit testing. This also simplifies unit testing of A (see chapter 4).

5.3.2 Subsystem Integration

The examples we used above describe how to integrate and test two classes. If paired classes behave as expected, they can then be treated as a new, compound component which can in turn be integrated with other classes. This way, step-by-step integration is used to create a cluster of classes that functions in perfect harmony. Such clusters are often referred to as packages or subsystems. The type of interface used by a cluster depends on the programming language being used. Some languages allow the separate specification of a package-specific interface, while others use the sum of the APIs of all classes within the cluster.

It is always preferable to use a package interface if possible. Just as we differentiate between `public` and `private` methods on a class level, a package-specific interface is encapsulated and keeps the number of externally usable methods to a minimum, thus also enhancing testability. Once they have been successfully tested, subsystems created this way can also be treated as individual components.

If a cluster of classes has been integrated to form a subsystem, the entire system can be seen on a higher level of abstraction as a set of subsystems. This approach allows us to conceptually treat hundreds of classes as a system that consists of perhaps a dozen subsystems that can each be subjected to separate unit tests. The required test cases can be directly derived from the unit and integration test cases used to test the subsystem's externally visible API methods. As with conventional class integration, subsystems can themselves be integrated to form new, increasingly complex subsystems or a complete system, and the required integration test cases can be derived and implemented the same way as they can for simple classes.

5.3.3 System Integration

Once all the subsystems have been successfully integrated and tested, the final step in the integration process is system integration. Unlike all the previous steps, this step involves checking that the complete product uses the intended interfaces to communicate as planned with the surrounding environment. These tests are performed for the most part as part of system testing (see chapter 6) within the system environment, and many projects do not differentiate between system test cases and system integration test cases.

Integrating a software system into a customer's own machines or some other custom device can be extremely tricky because it is difficult to simulate the target hardware sufficiently well within the system test environment. Although this step theoretically only involves installing the software (a process in which parameterization and system approval take priority), it often actually means performing an (additional) system test within the functional environment. This is a serious impediment for a Scrum Team, as the planned shippable product shouldn't require anything more than simple parameterization once it is installed at the customer site.

If the product reveals undiscovered defects once it is installed, the team will have to invest in extending the test environment and/or simulators. If these steps are not taken, instead of getting defect-free software, the customer will regularly receive software that is virtually guaranteed to contain defects and, from the customer's point of view, using Scrum methodology will have been a waste of time.

---

eHome Controller Case Study 5-4: System integration   *Case Study 5–4*

a) Successful system integration
The eHome system is installed by a technician at the customer site. Once it is installed, the technician parameterizes the system so that the house bus devices are all correctly identified and allocated within the system. The technician then runs the diagnostics program included with the package and, once it has finished successfully, takes the customer on a tour of the house, demonstrating the functionality of the wall switches and smartphone control of all major devices along the way.

b) Failed system integration
The customer uses a bus system that is new to the eHome team, and the bus adapter is written based on the specifications provided. However, the new bus system was not available during the manufacturer's own internal system test but a system is nevertheless delivered to the customer who ends up angrily canceling the purchase because the technician cannot get the system to work.

5.4 Traditional Integration Strategies

Traditionally managed projects usually perform integration and integration testing after unit (component) testing (see fig. 2-3). The assumption is that all software components have already been implemented and successfully unit tested before the integration phase begins. The integration team then takes subsets of grouped components, installs them in the integration environment and tests them. If the tests are successful, the subsystem in question is classified as integrated. If the tests fail, the defective component has to be reworked.

Although the system architecture determines which components belong to which subsystem, it is theoretically possible to organize the integration sequence as you wish. According to [Spillner/Linz 14], this can take place using one of the following basic strategies:

■ **Top-down Integration:**
Integration begins with a component that calls other components but is itself called only by the operating system.

■ **Bottom-up Integration:**
Testing begins with elemental components that do not call any others (except for operating system functions).

■ **Ad-hoc Integration:**
Components are integrated as and when they are completed by the programmers.

Pure top-down and bottom-up integration techniques require the system architecture to be designed on the basis of a tree diagram. The more cross-linked the basic architecture, the more you will have to deviate from the basic integration strategy. Additionally—as also found in projects managed using the V-model—it is rare for all components to be ready and unit tested, and integration thus often begins while some components are still being implemented. This inevitably leads to the use of an ad-hoc integration strategy.

5.5 Continuous Integration

Scrum-based projects continually produce new or altered code components, so we have to consider how to deal with them. A strategy based on traditional methods demands that the team waits until all code-related tasks are done and then installs all changes made by all programmers in the test environment for integration testing at the end of the Sprint. This is, however, a clear contradiction of the basic Scrum objectives:

- Integration test feedback to the programmer is unnecessarily delayed. In the worst possible case, a programmer who changes some code on the first day of the Sprint has to wait until the last day of the Sprint to receive integration test feedback.
- Because integration tests can and do reveal defects, the team has to include the time taken to remedy them in its plan. This forces the Sprint to adhere to a fixed sequence of coding, unit testing, integration (testing) and defect correction.

The result is a "Water-Scrum-Fall"—a strictly phase-oriented cascading approach to the Sprint. To prevent this from happening, the team needs to use a better integration strategy, namely: Continuous Integration.

Continuous Integration (CI) is the next logical step in the development of an incremental integration strategy. Incremental integration means that every piece of code is installed in the integration environment and is integrated as soon as it is finished. New components are therefore not grouped with others that have not yet been integrated but are instead integrated in place of a previously integrated version within a central integration environment.

5.5.1   The CI Process

Alongside its central integration environment, the other most important aspect of CI is that it is fully automated. According to [Duvall et al. 07], the Continuous Integration process consists of the following steps and elements:

- **Central code repository:**
  The team manages its program code and automated tests in a shared central code repository. Code is version-managed and every programmer has to check his/her code into the repository either daily or, better still, after every change (i.e., as often as possible).
- **Automated integration run:**
  Checking code into the repository automatically triggers an integration process that takes place on a dedicated CI server and consists of the following steps:

- **Compilation**

  The code is compiled, and compiler warnings and error messages are logged on the CI server. Compilation runs usually take a number of seconds.

- **Static code analysis**

  Successful compilation is followed by static code analysis that checks that the team has stuck to its own coding guidelines and quality metrics. These results are also logged on the CI server. Here too, a typical run takes a number of seconds. It is essential that the team only uses coding guidelines that can be checked automatically. No guidelines are to be drafted for code attributes that cannot be checked automatically or ones that the team considers to be insignificant.

- **Deployment to the test environment**

  Once the code has been compiled and statically checked, it can be deployed to and installed in the appropriate test environment, which is reset to a predefined state first.

- **Initialization**

  All initialization steps—such as creation and filling of database tables—take place automatically. The test data required for the tests that follow is also imported at this stage.

- **Unit testing**

  Automated unit tests for all units follow. The results are logged on the CI server.

- **Integration testing**

  Next up are automated integration tests. The results are logged on the CI server.

- **System testing**

  Finally, automated system tests are started. These results, too, are logged on the CI server. System tests can last up to several hours and are therefore not part of every CI run. They are usually run daily, normally during the night.

- **Feedback and dashboard:**

  The CI server displays all results on a central browser-based dashboard that gives immediate feedback in the case of test failures or other issues. Feedback is also pushed actively to the programmer(s) concerned via e-mail or other means.

Figure 5-4 (after [Duvall et al. 07], with additional test environments) shows a schematic of a typical CI environment.

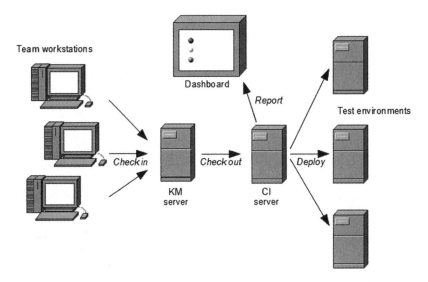

Fig. 5–4

A CI environment

The results of each step are displayed on the dashboard as they occur, not at the end of the complete CI run. The speed of the feedback loop to the team depends on how long each CI step takes. Compilation and static analysis typically take seconds or minutes to complete, while unit and integration testing usually takes a number of minutes. In contrast, system testing usually takes several hours. The CI server logs all test results and displays them in summarized form on a dashboard, keeping the entire team informed of the state of each CI run and the overall quality of the system. Figure 5-5 shows the dashboard used by the test*Bench* team (see case study 8.2).

The CI dashboard

Test Statistics Grid

Job	Success #	%	Failed #	%	Skipped #	%	Total #
● iTB Integration Tests	970	100%	0	0%	0	0%	970
● iTB Packaging	0	0%	0	0%	0	0%	0
● iTB REST Tests	18	100%	0	0%	0	0%	18
● iTB Static Analysis	0	0%	0	0%	0	0%	0
● iTB Nightly 2	662	<100%	2	>0%	0	0%	664
● iTB Utilities	1320	100%	0	0%	0	0%	1320
● iTEP Export Plugin	5	100%	0	0%	0	0%	5
● iTEP4	548	100%	0	0%	0	0%	548
● iTORX	5	100%	0	0%	0	0%	5
● Word Reporting	163	98%	0	0%	3	2%	166
Total	**3691**	**<100%**	**2**	**>0%**	**3**	**>0%**	**3696**

Test suites overview

■ Failed (0%) ■ Passed (100%) □ Skipped (0%)

■ iTB-unit-tests	0	997	0	997	100%
■ iTB-integration-tests_ORACLE	0	2936	0	2936	100%
■ iTB-integration-tests_MSSQL	0	2936	0	2936	100%
■ iTEP tests	0	548	0	548	100%

Fig. 5–5

A CI dashboard, showing

some typical results

5.5.2   Implementing CI

Technically speaking, CI is not a revolution. Software developers have always automated compilation runs using scripts, and most projects use configuration management systems to manage source code. Many projects also make automated nightly builds and, if the project manager is serious about quality, performs static code analysis on the nightly build too.

If a team already works this way, all it has to do to hit full CI is automate all tests and include them in the CI process. In contrast, a team that works according to only a few (or none) of the guidelines listed above will be faced with a steep learning curve. For the reasons listed at the beginning of section 5.5, it is not a good idea to ignore CI or delay its introduction.

Seen from a different angle, configuration management in many projects could be improved and the processes aren't nearly as highly automated as they could be, so introducing Scrum presents a real opportunity for a team to improve its integration process and the quality of its work.

Prepare the CI environment before the first Sprint

Introducing CI may involve a complete reorganization of the team's software repository, so the CI environment needs to be prepared before the start of the very first Sprint. This applies to all tools and can also affect the file system structure for the source code and its associated tests. It goes without saying that the scripts used to automate the CI process have to be written and tested too. As soon as the first Sprint begins and the programmers start work on their appointed tasks, the system has to be ready for code to be checked out, altered, checked back in and tested. The following are the steps we recommend when building up a CI environment:

▪ **Check the current state of the configuration management system**
Which configuration management (CM) tool is currently in use? How broadly is it implemented? Are there team members or sub-projects that use a different (or no) tool? If yes, why? How do the team members find the tool's handling? Simple? Complicated? How quickly can a build be compiled? Where or on which machine does the tool run? Is it centrally managed or does the team control the tool and the repository? Are there alternative (or better) tools available? The answers to all these questions can be found quickly and easily in a team workshop, as can a wish-list for all the parts of the CM system that could and should be improved to make it quicker, simpler and more reliable.

Getting to know CI tools
While it is checking the CM system, the team can also start to look at the CI server software that is available ([URL: Testtoolreview] is a good place to start). A CI server is a script-driven software tool that controls the individual steps involved in the CI process—for example, triggering and monitoring a compiler run, or the creation of a test package and logging the results. Experienced programmers can, of course, build their own tools using shell scripts, although today's CI server software provides ready-made scripts for all the important steps and a browser-based dashboard for outputting the results. The best approach is to hold a workshop in which team members can share the results of their research and demonstrate trial installations of the tools they have found.

Checking the current system and exchanging information within the team is the best way to gain acceptance for a new CI environment. The Scrum Master needs to be involved in the process too, as an inadequate CI environment can be a serious impediment. It is one of the first real tests of a new Scrum Master's mettle to build a great CI environment. Implementing the CI system involves these steps:

Choosing CM and CI tools
If the team decides to replace the current CM tool, the new tool has to work well with the chosen CI server software. A CI server has to reliably identify changes in code within the CM system so that it can be checked out and set up for inclusion in a CI run.

Installing CM and CI tools
The selected tools should be installed on a separate computer, which also has to be acquired if necessary. It makes no sense to install CM and CI tools on a development machine. Make sure that all parts of the system are covered by appropriate backup systems.

Migrating CM
The old code repository needs to be imported into the new CM system. Any changes to the file system that this requires can involve a lot of effort and are sure to be prone to errors.

CI scripting
The CI scripts delivered with the software have to be adapted to work in the project environment. Start with the scripts that monitor the code repository for changes before checking the latest code out for import to the compiler.

At this point, the team has the minimum functionality that it needs to begin work. The programmers can check code into the central repository, and the system automatically makes a new build. This checks that new code is compilable (i.e., it is complete and syntactically correct). At this stage, the system is similar to a conventional CM system but doesn't yet include any automated tests.

The appropriate automated test packages now have to be adapted and installed. This usually takes place gradually in the form of specific test package tasks that are planned in the course of the Sprints that follow. The following points describe the degree of automation that you should aim to achieve:

- Every build is immediately subject to automated unit tests. This is a realistic target if the team is disciplined in its use of test-driven development (see chapter 4). If the team has already created automated unit tests, these can be imported into the new CI system. The test source code and test data have to be version managed within the CM system.
- Integration tests are added. It can sometimes be useful to move integration test cases that are part of existing unit tests packages to a separate integration test package. From this point onward, the team needs to consider the type of environment the integration tests will need and whether it makes sense to perform unit tests in a simpler, faster environment. If the team decides to separate the test environments, it will have to draft tasks for the creation of new, more complex scripts and the setup of the new environment(s).
- System tests, too, can be largely automated and included in the CI system, provided the team extends its use of Test First principles (see chapter 6) beyond unit and integration testing to cover system testing as well.

A CI environment cannot be built on the fly. Setting up a CI environment is a complex task that shouldn't be taken lightly. CI has to be carefully planned (case study 8.2 provides a step-by-step example), and the setup phase can take several weeks, during which normal product development activities cannot be pursued.

Even if the CI environment is up and running, it cannot be guaranteed to produce defect-free builds (see [Pichler/Roock 11, section 4.10]). For example, if no static code analysis was performed before making the switch to CI, the first few analyses thrown up by the build process will be full of warnings and error messages, even for components and code segments that the team has already classified as stable and done. In such cases, the team will either have to soften its code analysis rules or rework all of the affected code. Due to the sudden increase in test coverage, the same thing happens when unit and integration tests are run for the first time. Even if the same tests have already been run successfully on individual developers' machines, the results they produce can look very different when they are run in a centrally managed CI environment.

While CI is being implemented, the team will appear to the outside world and the Product Owner to be less productive than it was before Scrum was introduced. This can be a sobering experience that leads to disappointment on the part of some team members. It is the Scrum Master's job to protect the team from unwarranted criticism and to support it while it is getting set up.

5.5.3   Optimizing CI

A CI run has to test the system as comprehensively as possible within the shortest possible timespan. To balance out these apparently conflicting requirements, the team can:

- **Create batches of tests**
  The distinction between static analysis and unit, integration and system tests separates tests into broad categories which can be broken down into smaller batches as necessary. Smaller batches of tests not only guarantee that the test run stops sooner when it fails, but also enable you to use or hide them depending on the needs of the current situation. For example, if you only include the batches that address code that has been altered since the previous run, you can save a lot of time during testing (especially system testing). However, the tradeoff for a shorter runtime is an increased risk of overlooking altered code and leaving out the required batch of tests.

- **Halt the test run**
  You have to decide whether to continue running a batch (or batches) of tests when a single test fails. In many cases, subsequent tests require certain basic object behaviors if they are to run at all, and a failed test can preclude this. A halted run is, of course, shorter and means that the CI server's full capacity is available sooner for the next attempt. On the other hand, because the data that would have resulted from later tests is missing, it can make debugging and defect correction more difficult. We can also speculate that subsequent tests might reveal other defects that could be remedied too, which would be really annoying. The

scripts that control the CI process need to include a consistent start/ stop strategy agreed on by the team in advance.

Parallelize tests

Another way to accelerate testing processes is to run batches of tests in parallel, resulting in a CI run that only lasts as long as it takes to run the largest batch. However, running tests in parallel can be quite tricky for a number of reasons:

- Parallel batches of tests need to be independent of each other. In other words, no test included in batch B can rely on objects that are affected by running batch A. This requires careful construction of the test batches and the inclusion of appropriately modular test cases within each batch.
- The system being tested must allow parallel access and processing at the test interface. If this is not the case, the test will either be serialized by the test object or it will fail. The tests themselves have to be written in a way that enables them to run in a parallel test environment. If this is not the case, test results might overwrite each other and it will be impossible to tell which log entries were produced by which test.

Parallelize the test environment

Instead of running multiple tests on a single object, it is generally easier to install the test object multiple times (for example, on multiple virtual machines) and distribute the test batches between the various environments. Such a system could, for example, run unit and simple integration tests in environment #1, complex integration tests in environment #2, and system tests in environment #3. This way, each environment can be run using bespoke hard- and software specified for the particular task at hand. This can increase the required hardware budget but makes testing much more efficient. For example, any systems that use databases require the affected database(s) and all the related test data to be installed for system testing. Setting up such a test database involves a lot of effort and results in relatively slow data access, so lower level tests are often performed using a simple substitute database that resides in the system's RAM. Such a setup is easier to install and runs faster too.

Upgrade the test hardware

Using more or faster hardware is an obvious way to accelerate the CI process. Unfortunately, this simple step cannot be taken for granted and, rather than spending $1,000 on faster hardware, many companies prefer to recruit a member of another team for a week to perform tasks such as optimizing a shell script's runtime.

A slow CI process is a serious impediment. If the system runs slowly, it is tempting to hide batches of tests or even avoid checking in new code to speed things up. If the team's work suffers due to something as banal as the effect of using slow hardware, it is up to the Scrum Master to help cure the deficit.

Maintenance and optimization of the CI environment and reducing testing time are perpetual challenges. CI optimization issues should be a regular part of the team's retrospectives and need to be included in its Sprint Planning activity. For each Sprint, the Scrum Master and the Product Owner have to decide how best to divide resources between short-term feature productivity and mid-term improvements to the CI system that help to increase overall team productivity.

Continuous optimization of the CI environment

5.6   Integration Test Management

The most important aspect of integration test management is ensuring that sufficient numbers of appropriate test cases are written and run. The similarities between unit and integration tests sometimes make it difficult for programmers to identify which integration tests are missing and which need to be added.

Integration test cases have to be geared toward the system's basic architecture, so the testers involved have to have a clear idea of the structure of the planned architecture. On the other hand, integration tests check the degree to which the actual architecture represents the planned one. Integration tests can and should be designed using the Test First principle and are a useful tool for specifying the system architecture and checking its development during subsequent Sprints. The team's test manager can use Test First to push the process of architectural development forward and can also use the results of integration tests to help the team update the system's architecture—for example, by simplifying interfaces, defining subsystems, identifying and remedying performance bottlenecks, etc. The results of discussing such issues will represent the team's collective opinion of the target system architecture and as such, need to be re-drafted regularly—either graphically in the form of architecture diagrams or as automated Test First integration test cases. If the team doesn't follow this route, the result will be a bottom-up system that contains a great many (more or less) randomly structured classes.

In a Scrum environment, the integration strategy is largely defined by the Story Map (see chapter 3) and, in the case of individual Sprints, by the Sprint Backlog, which determines which features are to be implemented during which Sprint and thus which components are finished when. Because every component is integrated immediately (or continuously) into the system, Sprint Planning also determines the integration test sequence in advance. It is therefore important to consider the integration sequence that the Story Map dictates while deciding who should deal with which tasks during a Sprint. If it possible to choose, you should always select the sequence for the forthcoming tasks that entails the least possible integration effort.

Take integration testing effort into account during Sprint Planning.

The effort involved in designing, automating and updating integration tests must be taken into account by the test manager during Sprint Planning. The effort involved doesn't scale directly in relation to the number of changed or new components, but rather to the number of dependencies between them, and can be disproportionately high as a result. Setting up the test environment and developing placeholders also involves a lot of additional effort. However, all this effort is necessary to ensure that the integration process for every component can be automatically and continuously executed following every change in the code.

During the CI process, the test manager also has to check whether additional integration-related code analysis is possible—for example, to statically check interfaces for consistency and adherence to their abstract specifications[5] or checking that the required files and messages are available in the appropriate formats[6]. Attention also has to be paid to sorting automated integration tests into batches and the continuous optimization of the speed of the CI process.

---

5. Based on formal interface and service definition languages such as IDL [URL: OMG] and WDSL [URL: W3C].
6. Using syntax validation tools for HTML pages or CSS definitions [URL: W3C validator].

5.7   Questions and Exercises

5.7.1   Self-Assessment

Questions and exercises to help you assess how agile your project or team really is.

1.   Does the team have and use automated integration tests? How many? How many of these are related to unit test cases?
2.   Where and how is the system architecture defined and documented? Do the existing integration test cases check that this architecture is implemented?
3.   Is there a review process for comparing the test cases with the actual architecture? Does this take place regularly? What conclusions does it draw?
4.   Which interfaces are covered by integration tests? What degree of coverage is achieved?
5.   What are the target coverage values? How often are these values measured?
6.   Which values have been achieved now/today? Where does the team store these values? Where can they be found if I want to know them now?
7.   Which measures have been introduced to improve test coverage and/or the quality of integration tests?
8.   Do we use interface monitors? For which interfaces?
9.   Is there an automated CI process? If yes, how is it structured?
10.   When are integration tests performed? Are they part of the CI environment?
11.   In which test environment is integration testing performed? Is this environment adequately defined, and can it be reliably reproduced?
12.   How does the duration of integration testing compare with that of unit testing?
13.   When are integration tests designed? Based on a description of the system architecture? Before coding begins (Test First)? As soon as a component is finished? Or at the end of the Sprint?
14.   Are integration tasks planned explicitly as part of the Sprint Backlog?
15.   Are integration tests part of the Definition of Done?
16.   How do the results of the existing integration tests look now/today?

17. How many of which types of defects do the integration tests reveal compared to the unit tests?

18. How are defect management and bug fixing performed if subsystem interfaces written by other teams are defective?

19. How are agreements about inter-team interfaces documented? Is this issue discussed during the Scrum of Scrums?

20. Which other architecture and interface-related checks does the team perform? Architecture reviews? Automatic analysis? Validation of interfaces and data?

21. Are the CI process and its results discussed during the Daily Scrum?

22. Are ways to improve the CI process discussed during retrospectives? What is the current state of this discussion? What specific measures have been agreed upon? Which of these are being worked on in the current Sprint?

23. If multiple teams are working on the same project, do they use a shared CI process? Who is responsible for it? Who do the CI tools and hardware "belong to"? Is this issue discussed during the Scrum of Scrums?

5.7.2 Methods and Techniques

These questions will help you to review the content of the current chapter.

1. What are the most typical types of integration failures? Explain their causes and symptoms.

2. How can integration tests be systematically derived? Name and describe the necessary steps.

3. Explain the similarities and differences between a unit test case and an integration test case.

4. When are two software components dependent on each other? What are the differences between explicit and implicit dependencies?

5. Explain the term "testability."

6. How and why does the testability of an interface affect the effort involved in its corresponding integration tests?

7. Why are integration tests especially important in object-oriented systems?

8. How does the iterative Scrum approach to projects increase the effort involved in integration testing?

9. Why might refactoring the system architecture reduce the effort involved in integration testing?
10. Name the different types of class integration.
11. What is subsystem integration?
12. What is system integration?
13. Explain how Sprint Planning can affect the integration test sequence.
14. Which elements and processes are part of the CI process?
15. "No CI, no Scrum!" Discuss this statement.
16. Which steps have to be taken when implementing a CI process?
17. What steps can be taken to continually optimize the CI process?

5.7.3 Other Exercises

These exercises will help you delve deeper into topics touched on in the course of the chapter.

1. Explain which types of integration defects can and cannot be discovered using syntax checks during compilation.
2. What types of integration failures only occur in asynchronously coupled components? Why?
3. What is the effect of unintentionally coupling an asynchronous component synchronously? Explain the differences in behavior this produces by means of an eHome roller blind control command. How might a test look that checks whether such a command is performed asynchronously?
4. Software components can be directly or indirectly dependent. Describe some typical sources of indirect dependencies.
5. Explain how implicit dependency can be transformed into explicit dependency. Give an example.
6. Assume that three components use the same file as a resource. Explain why negative tests and robustness tests for these components involve more effort than when the file is encapsulated in a centrally managed service. Why is this not the case for positive or Happy Path tests?

6   System Testing and Testing Nonstop

In addition to unit and integration testing, system testing is an essential part of every agile project. This chapter explains what system tests are and the demands they make on the test environment. We examine the various points during a Sprint that are suitable for performing system tests, and we also discuss the specifically agile aspects of system testing as well as exploratory and acceptance testing.

6.1   System Testing

Scrum aims to produce a potentially shippable product at the end of every Sprint. Such a product has to be capable of running outside of the CI environment, has to have a user interface and usually has to be capable of interacting with the customer's other systems. System tests check that the system works from the user's point of view using the customer's own interfaces. For system tests to be effective, they have to be performed in an environment that emulates the end-user environment as precisely as possible.

Neither unit tests nor integration tests are capable of doing this, so we have to create and apply system tests that check the aspects of the system that unit and integration testing don't cover. Let's use our case study as an example:

System testing checks aspects of the product that unit and integration testing do not cover.

---

eHome Controller Case Study 6-1: System test cases

If the user opens the eHome Controller in a browser and clicks the "kitchen lamp" button to switch it on, the expectation is that the real-world lamp on the ceiling switches on, too. The corresponding system test therefore has to guarantee that:

1. Based on the existing acceptance criteria, the system fulfills the requirements drafted in the Backlog.

2. The entire functional chain—from the user interface to the physical act of switching on the device—has to be tested for complete functionality.

Case Study 6–1

The team's test manager formulates the following system test cases (STs) based on the eHome Controller Backlog (see section 3.3):

ST-1: Device control

ST-1.1: Switch the kitchen lamp on/off. Check that the switching action takes place and that it is visualized in the browser.

ST-1.2: Switch the dimmable living room lamp on, starting at 50% brightness, then raise to 70% and then dim to 30%. Check each step in the actuator and in the browser interface. Dim to 0% and check that the device status switches to off.

ST-1.3: Close the living room blind and then re-open it. Check that the blind and its actuator react correctly and that the action is confirmed and visualized in the browser.

ST-2: Switching programs

ST-2.1: Program the following actions: Tilt the blinds on weekdays at 7am; raise all south-facing blinds at 8:30 am; close all blinds at 8:30pm.

ST-3: Fetch sensor data.

ST-3.1: Retrieve "Living room temperature" value by clicking on the corresponding sensor icon in the browser.

ST-3.2: Trigger the "storm" message from the wind sensor and check that the corresponding "raise all blinds" command is executed.

The test environment has to fulfill certain preconditions (ENVs) if the tests listed above are to be performed successfully—for example:

ENV-1: The device running the browser has to locate the eHome Controller on the network and be capable of communicating with it.

ENV-2: The controller has to relay the commands produced by clicking browser icons to the correct actuators. To do this, the controller has to know which icon represents which physical actuator/device. The appropriate device data has to be correctly entered and parameterized in the eHome Controller database (see fig. 3-2 on page 31).

ENV-3: The eHome Controller has to be able to contact all actuators/ devices via the system bus. A bus adapter that corresponds to the bus protocol has to be installed.

ENV-4: Every actuator has to understand the commands it receives and act on them. To do this, every actuator has to be correctly parameterized and correctly (physically) wired.

ENV-5: All switchable devices have to be either correctly wired up to the corresponding actuators or adequately simulated by display elements or measuring instruments.

Our example shows clearly that system tests check the entire functional chain. A system test case triggers a flow of data that passes through the entire system—from the user interface via the bus to the actuator and back. This type of test is often referred to as an end-to-end test[1]. The places where test data are controlled and observed (Points of Control and Observation) represent the places where the end-user takes note of the functionality (or non-functionality) of the product.

End-to-end testing

System test cases can be derived directly from the requirements and acceptance criteria listed in the Product Backlog or from corresponding use case descriptions. The team should not, however, take these sources as read and should actively seek gaps in the documentation and attempt to draft new variations and special cases as well as additional foreseeable use cases.

Check against requirements to discover gaps in the system

The dialog with the Product Owner should be used to clarify when and whether requirements listed in the Backlog need to be more precisely defined (based on input from the testers[2]) and whether additional requirements need to be drafted and added to the Backlog.

---

eHome Controller Case Study 6-2: Backlog update based on system test feedback

Case Study 6–2

ST-3.2 is a system test case that has no equivalent requirement in the Backlog.

However, the team and the Product Owner know that the system incorporates a number of additional sensors (among others, for wind and light) that issue alarms when a user-definable threshold value is reached. The eHome owner obviously expects the system to react to these, so a new requirement is added to the Backlog (see section 3.3):

Topic	Priority	Description / *Acceptance criteria*
React to alarms		A sensor can be assigned to one or more switching programs that are activated when the bus adapter receives and reads an alarm message.
	2	☐ *The "storm" signal from a wind sensor triggers the preprogrammed "raise all blinds" command.*
	3	☐ *The command program starts a maximum of one second after the alarm message is received.*

---

1. Not every system test has to be designed as an end-to-end test.
2. A reference to the corresponding test cases is often sufficient.

6.2   The System Testing Environment

System testing usually requires a more complex environment than unit or integration testing—a situation that is well illustrated by the various eHome test environments described here and in the previous two chapters. A system testing environment has to realistically emulate the real-world environment at the customer site and is designed to check that the system doesn't only work in the lab. The more realistic the test environment, the more likely it is that a failure-free, system-tested product will also work perfectly when installed in the customer's own environment. Conversely, a system test environment that is too simple increases the risk of undiscovered issues causing problems once the product has been installed.

Similarity of the system testing environment to the production environment

The test environment needs to reproduce the production environment as accurately as possible. This means that external components that the product will work with in the end-user environment have to be represented within the test environment, either by real components or realistic simulations. Instead of test drivers and placeholders, the maximum possible number of real-world components (such as computer hardware, system software, drivers, networks and other systems) needs to be installed in the test environment. A complete system testing environment can end up being extremely complex (and expensive).

The large number of components involved also means that there is a large number of different ways in which they can be set up and configured. There are a number of typical configurations used by specific user groups, for specific usage scenarios or for certain compatibility attributes of the product being tested.

Case Study 6–3

eHome Controller Case Study 6-3: System test environment

The requirement "runs in Firefox 15.0 or later" listed in the Product Backlog (see section 3.3) is not covered by a test case but instead by the test environment itself, where Firefox 15.0 (and selected newer versions including the latest) is installed on the test client computer.

The requirement "All eHome Tools devices can be controlled via the eHome Tools adapter" is covered by the fact that all currently available eHome Tools bus devices are set up as part of the test environment and are connected via a central bus.

The compatibility with third-party devices is tested using similar setups that include the required devices.

The effort involved in system testing does not scale according to the num-   *System testing effort*
ber of system test cases, but rather with the number of different test envi-
ronments that need to be checked for functionality. What effects does this
have on agile projects?

- The list of materials and the configuration of the system testing environment have to be carefully planned and defined, and only then is it
  clear how meaningful the test results are. However, you still have to
  strike the right compromise between the usefulness of the results and
  the cost of the environment used to produce them.
- The initial setup of a system test environment can be a complex, costly
  and error-prone undertaking. Tasks that deal with setting up the system test environment need to be included in early Sprints. If they are
  not, the team runs the risk of receiving system testing feedback at too
  late a stage in the project (see section 6.8.1).
- Test environment maintenance time has to be reserved in every Sprint.
  If you don't take time to maintain the test environment, it will quickly
  become obsolete and create serious impediments. System configuration will no longer keep pace with product development and any new
  configurations that new features require will not be implemented. The
  result will be system tests that become less and less meaningful or that
  can no longer be executed as the Sprints progress.
- The large number of heterogeneous components involved make it difficult to automate the setup and configuration of the system test environment, but it is nevertheless worth the effort. Here too, you have to
  make sure that you plan regular environment automation tasks.
- The Scrum Master should use Retrospectives (see section 7.2.3) to
  address the options available for optimizing the (system) testing environment. However, the optimization steps necessary for unit, integration and system testing environments vary significantly. Unit and integration test environments are designed for maximum speed and each
  test case checks just one small element of the system under deliberately
  simplified conditions (for example, sending a switching command and
  writing the result to a file). External components such as the eHome
  bus or switch actuators are replaced for unit testing by placeholders
  (see chapter 4). System tests, too, should run as quickly as possible, but
  the meaningfulness of the results takes priority over the speed at which
  they are produced. These differences in the aims of the various types of
  tests make it necessary to build separate testing environments for each.

The cost of setting up a system testing environment means that it often has to be shared between teams or development units. This can make task planning more difficult and can mean that a team has to coordinate testing slots with other teams or perform system tests at predetermined times. The Scrum Master is responsible for coordinating test slots, usually during the Scrum of Scrums [URL: Scrum Guide].

6.3 Manual System Testing

6.3.1 Exploratory Testing

Exploratory testing is a popular agile approach to testing and combines investigation of the system that is to be tested with the design and performance of manual tests (see [Crispin/Gregory 08]). The most important features of this approach are:

- At the start of a session, the tester defines only the objectives of the test—i.e., which feature or User Story is to be tested. The session that follows concentrates on this single aspect of the product. The overall structure of the test and the individual steps it involves are not specified in advance.

- The tester then attempts to execute the Story or feature concerned and observes the system's behavior.

- To ascertain whether the test object works as intended, the tester uses all available information that is considered useful and relevant to the object being tested. This information might be the task card that briefly describes the feature or any other kind of information. Scarce or missing documentation is counterbalanced by active exploration of the system being tested.

- The structure of the test and the route taken through the system depends on the observations the tester makes during the session. Software components that behave normally or that are already known are skipped or given a quick test. Where "smells" are discovered (i.e., places where the software behaves in a way the tester doesn't expect), the tests are expanded to divine the reasons for the malfunction.

- Observations, queries, warnings, conclusions and questions for the programmer(s) are noted immediately.

The tester doesn't require a detailed specification for the test object or the test. The test is created while it is being performed and concentrates on suspect or defective components. This approach is perfect for taking a quick look at new or unknown features.

Ideal for checking new features quickly

On the downside, the quality of an exploratory test depends heavily on the tester's degree of discipline, level of experience, and feel for the software. Such tests are difficult or impossible to reproduce and have to be performed manually. Exploratory testers also run the risk of drifting off course, which is then reflected in a correspondingly low rate of defect detection.

6.3.2   Session-Based Testing

Session-based testing attempts to mitigate some of the disadvantages of exploratory testing. The most important features of this approach are:

- The tester describes the objectives of the test and its strategy in two or three short sentences.
- The test session itself is timeboxed to last a maximum of 90 minutes that are divided into setup, test design and execution, defect localization and defect reporting phases.
- A session sheet is created that records in note form the aim of the test, details of the system being tested, details of the procedure, test coverage, short descriptions of the functions and interface elements tested, defects that are discovered, unanswered questions, etc. The idea here is that the contents of all the available session sheets can be electronically condensed and analyzed.

Session-based testing utilizes all the advantages of exploratory testing and places the procedure within a formalized framework. The electronic test logs thus produced are a real boon and can be used to reliably reproduce tests and enable the team to analyze all similar tests using the same criteria. Using session sheet notation based on keywords helps to build a reliable basis for long-term test automation (see also section 6.4: Automated System Testing).

Session-based testing is also a useful tool with which the Product Owner and the customer (or perhaps usability specialists) can quickly gain an impression of the current state of the product and how end-users deal with it. Experience has shown that if a tester takes part in such sessions, the lessons learned can be better logged and reproduced.

6.3.3   Acceptance Testing

Agile software development literature often refers only to unit testing and user acceptance testing, creating the impression that automated unit tests and manual, exploratory acceptance tests make the integration tests and system tests familiar to users of the V-model superfluous. Some authors ([Crispin/Gregory 08], for example[3]) use the terms "acceptance testing" and "system testing" synonymously. But not every acceptance test case is equivalent to a system test case, and unit test cases and integration test cases can be used as part of an acceptance test suite.

Did we build the right system?

The ISTQB glossary [URL: ISTQB Glossary] defines an acceptance test as one that, "… enables the user, customer or other authorized entity to determine whether or not to accept the system." Acceptance tests can therefore be seen as approval tests that the customer or the customer's representative (in Scrum, the Product Owner) selects and performs to gain approval for the shipped product. Here, the aim is to question whether the product fulfills its intended use and provides the right functionality ("Did we build the right system?"). In Scrum, the acceptance criteria for every feature are agreed on by the team and the Product Owner and are recorded in the Backlog. The translation of these criteria into appropriate (manual or automated) test cases takes place during the Sprint.

Did we build the system right?

Because the Product Owner represents the customer within the Scrum Team, acceptance tests can be seen as a quality assurance (QA) tool that primarily serves the Product Owner, whereas unit, integration and system tests are a QA tool that serves the team ("Did we build the system right?"). Although the customer/Product Owner and the team use tests to achieve different aims, the contents of acceptance tests don't necessarily differ too much from that of the team's own tests. The team can apply the steps described in an acceptance test for tests performed on a different level, just as the Product Owner can use the mass of existing system tests to derive parts of the acceptance test suite.

Manual acceptance tests supplement other automated tests.

In practice, a Sprint's acceptance testing will be limited to cover only the elements of the product that are newly created or altered during the Sprint. The team then demonstrates these acceptance test cases to the Product Owner during the Sprint Demo in the form of manual explor-

---

3. "Acceptance tests verify that all aspects of the system, including qualities such as usability and performance, meet customer requirements" [Crispin/Gregory 08, chapter 6].

atory tests. If all other tests are automated, this approach holds few risks. However, if no other system tests take place during the Sprint, it is more likely that unwanted side effects caused by changes made during the Sprint remain undiscovered.

6.4   Automated System Testing

In Scrum Projects, unit and integration tests are usually performed automatically using xUnit test scripts. If these test scripts are embedded in the CI environment, they are automatically run every time the code is altered (see chapters 4 and 5). In effect, unit and integration tests are run continuously and deliver constant, timely feedback to the team.

It would be great if we could achieve a similar level of speed and convenience during system testing. However, the complex environment (see above) makes this difficult to achieve. Additionally, it is harder to automate system tests than it is to write xUnit tests, because:

- The most important system test interface is the product's GUI, which requires the use of dedicated GUI test tools (see [URL: Testtool-review]). These run a lot slower than typical xUnit tests. GUI tests also have to wait for reactions and signals from other components (such as a database) or external systems. GUI tests therefore run significantly slower than typical unit tests.
- The system configuration must have a clearly defined and reproducible original state that the test scripts can be reliably based on.
- Other interfaces often play a role, requiring appropriate additional tests and test automation tools.
- Test results often have to be analyzed manually because it is too difficult (or even impossible) to automatically compare expected behavior with actual behavior.
- For similar reasons, some system test cases might require manual intervention.
- And finally, the team has few or no members who are experienced in automating system tests.

6.4.1   Record/Playback Testing

Unit and integration test interfaces exist on a program code level. Test cases are created using xUnit so that each test case contributes to a single method of the test object's API, and the contents of each test case can be directly derived from the planned functionality of the API method. The vocabulary these tests are based on is derived from the API methods and their parameters. Things look different for system tests, which usually use the product's GUI as the main testing interface. System tests are thus written using the steps the user can take via the GUI as their basic vocabulary.

Record/playback tools record sequences of commands.

Record/playback tools are used to record sequences of user commands: A record/playback tool records all manually entered keyboard- and mouse-driven commands that the tester performs during a test session and saves them in the form of a script. Running the script reproduces the recorded test sequence—an action that can be repeated as often as necessary (after [Spillner/Linz 14]). A test script for our eHome case study could take shape as follows:

Case Study 6–4

eHome-Controller Case Study 6-4: System test command sequence

The tester starts the eHome Controller browser application and uses mouse clicks to switch the lamp near the kitchen window on and off. The corresponding browser window looks like this:

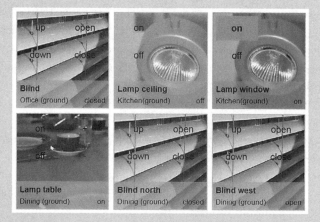

The tester captures the commands using the Selenium IDE record/playback tool (see [URL: Testtoolreview]), producing a test script that looks like this:

```
open http://ehome/eHomeController/index.php
clickAndWait xpath=(//a[contains(text(),'on')])[2]
clickAndWait xpath=(//a[contains(text(),'off')])[2]
```

This script only clicks the lamp's on/off button, and doesn't check whether the system actually performs the command. The test case expects an english-language user interface ("on", "off") in which the kitchen window lamp appears as a second lamp icon. It thus binds the test case tightly to the GUI and the test environment—in this case using the `clickAndWait` command, whose duration can vary depending on how the test environment is set up.

If you use a record/playback tool to record click-based system test cases, it is easy to fall into such traps. This approach also ties you to the use of a particular type of interface (in this case, HTML). However, the GUI is an element of the product that often changes significantly during the course of the project's Sprints, so the corresponding tests have to be constantly altered to fit the changing shape of the command structure and the GUI. Generally, it is preferable to spend time during a Sprint writing new tests for new product functions rather than constantly maintaining and updating existing tests. Another drawback of this approach is that it doesn't cater to alternative GUIs or GUI layouts. For example, the eHome Controller can be operated via a complex browser GUI or a simpler smartphone/tablet Web interface. It would take too much time and is simply not economical to create system tests for each available interface.

6.4.2 Keyword-Driven Testing

The team can avoid these issues if it uses a more abstract test vocabulary instead of describing the test procedure using system navigation commands. The best choice is usually the vocabulary associated with the system's use cases or business logic.

This is an established approach to system test creation known as keyword-driven testing. The eHome Controller's business logic revolves around switching electrical devices, and the eHome team decides to define a corresponding Domain Specific Language (DSL)[4] for the creation of its system tests:

---

4. This command/keyword notation can be seen as a simple Domain Specific Language (DSL). DSLs are an interesting test automation approach for use in Scrum projects. Complex DSLs have their own variables, control structures, procedure definitions and other syntactic elements. Useful introductions to building DSLs can be found in [Ghosh 11], [Fowler/Parsons 10] and [Rahien 10]. The basics of compiler building are discussed in [Aho et al. 06].

Case Study 6–5a

eHome Controller Case Study 6-5a: Developing a system testing DSL

The eHome owner uses the eHome software to control electrical devices (e.g., lamps) or to display the status of various sensors (e.g., room temperature). Lamps can be switched on and off or dimmed, while sensors can be read and given specific threshold values.

Sentences using a simple language, constructed using these objects within this domain, can thus be built according to the pattern <object_name> <command> and might look like this:

```
switch kitchen lamp on;
display living room temperature;
```

Fine-tuning the language allows us to be more precise about the device we wish to test:

```
<floor><room><object_type><object_name><command><parameter>
```

This simple formula is sufficient to describe relatively complex sequences of commands. For example, the owner of an eHome could enter the following commands into the smartphone interface during the journey home:

```
open garage door
living room heating 20 degrees
ground floor lamp on[a]
living room couch lamp dim 60%[b]
television on[c]
```

a.   If the object name is missing, all devices in a particular location will be activated.
b.   The parameters available depend on the command being used.
c.   If the object name is unique, the location doesn't need to be specified.

As you can see, our new DSL is well suited to noting use cases and, as a side effect, it also specifies a command-based user interface for the eHome Controller. To use it as a domain-specific testing language, we need to ensure that the system's reactions to these commands are correctly identified and are compared with the expected reactions. This means we have to add a check function to the actions listed above. A system test case could thus look like this:

Case Study 6–5b

eHome Controller Case Study 6-5b: System test case

Command syntax	Sequence control test function calls
kitchen window lamp on	switch('kitchen','lamp','window','on');
kitchen window lamp status? on	assert('kitchen','lamp','window','on');

The check command `assert` reads the status of the kitchen lamp and checks that it is on. Depending on how smart your parser and test sequence controller are (the sequence controller has to be capable of executing the commands you define), you can make the user interface and the test language as convenient to handle as you like. It is also helpful if the parameters you use can be represented by variables or tables of values:

---

eHome Controller Case Study 6-5c: Data-driven testing

Case Study 6–5c

```
switch (FLOOR, ROOM, DEVICE, NAME, 'off');ᵃ
assert (FLOOR, ROOM, DEVICE, NAME, 'off');
switch (FLOOR, ROOM, DEVICE, NAME, 'on');
assert (FLOOR, ROOM, DEVICE, NAME, 'on');
switch (FLOOR, ROOM, DEVICE, NAME, 'off');
```

FLOOR	ROOM	DEVICE	NAME
GF	living room	lamp	couch
GF	kitchen	lamp	window
FF	child	power outlet	television
...			

---

a. The on/off command can also be included in the test data table. However, the purpose of this test sequence is to check that a number of devices can be correctly switched on and off, and the purpose becomes clearer if the on/off command is coded into the test case rather than listed with the other test data.

A table of values is used to provide the test sequence listed above with appropriate test data, creating a data-driven test that switches the devices listed in the table on and off, checks whether the switching commands are executed and, finally, switches the status of each device back to off.

The advantages of a keyword-based, domain-specific testing language are:

The advantages of a keyword-based, domain-specific testing language

- Test cases are written exclusively using the language of the application domain. They represent what the system should be capable of but not how it works. They are easy to understand for testers, users, the customer and other interested parties and provide meaningful feedback to all those involved.
- Even if the implementation of the product changes, the tests remain valid and executable. The sample tests listed above can equally well be

used to test a PC browser interface or a completely different smartphone interface.

▪ Test cases written this way can also be used to control lower level system interfaces without having to rewrite them. In our example, a test driver could be used to translate the test cases into controller commands that can be fed directly to the eHome Controller. The test driver can serve as a placeholder for the GUI, enabling tests to be run without the GUI. This approach reduces the duration of the testing phase and enables us to test the Controller at the unit and integration testing stage, even if the GUI isn't yet complete.

This degree of convenience comes at a price. The team has to agree on a set of keywords that then has to remain stable, and has to write an interpreter to convert the resulting commands into appropriate function calls. It also has to create a sequence control mechanism to execute the commands and an adapter that connects the sequence control mechanism to the test object. To ensure that the adapter correctly identifies the various objects that need to be tested (in the case of our GUI, these are buttons, check boxes, radio buttons, text fields etc.), they all have to be given unique identifiers that remain the same throughout the course of the pending Sprints. If the identifiers change, the team will have to waste effort altering the test code from Sprint to Sprint. Figure 6-1 shows how the various levels of such an automated test system interact.

Fig. 6–1

Three-level test architecture

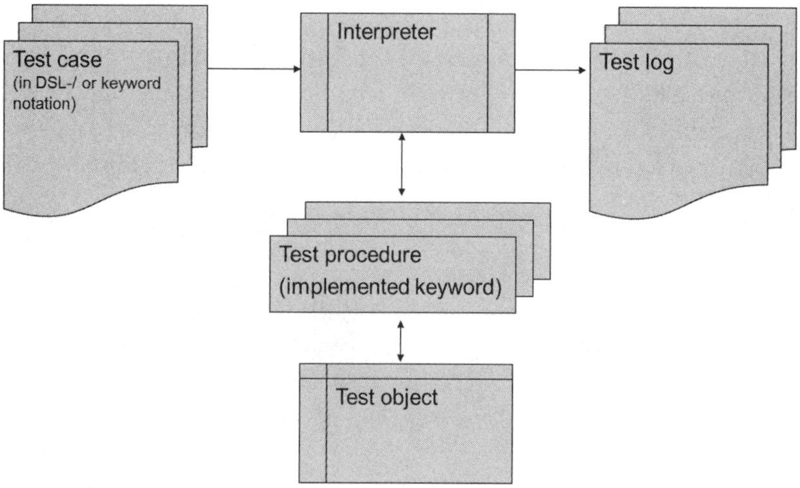

A three-level test architecture draws clear boundaries between the various tasks involved and hands over tasks that have nothing to do with test logic to the adapter or the test sequence control unit: *Three-level test architecture*

- **Decoupling the test environment**

  A parameter such as a timeout limit is not an attribute of the test case but rather of the runtime behavior of the test environment and should be transferred to test sequence control where it can be implemented as a method of a test environment class (`TestEnvironment`). When this method is called (for example, with `TestEnvironment->wait_for MsgAck()`), we can be sure that it only waits for an acknowledge signal for the amount of time stipulated by the test environment, and the time spent waiting is no longer an attribute of the test logic. Other test environment attributes can be diverted from the test logic in a similar way.

- **Decoupling the test interface**

  If the test logic becomes too intertwined with a particular test interface, the test can only be performed using that interface. Unlike unit and integration tests, some system tests need to be run through multiple interfaces. For example, the eHome Controller can be controlled via various interfaces (PC browsers, smartphone browsers and apps, and command-line interfaces). Because the test sequence controller accesses the desired interface indirectly via an adapter, it can communicate with other interfaces simply by swapping out the adapter without having to alter the test logic. The adapter translates the test steps into a form that the interface understands. To perform tests via the test object's GUI, you need to use an adapter that can control a corresponding record/playback tool (such as Selenium IDE) and translate commands into a form it can process.

While designing system tests, the team has to assess just how much modularity and flexibility the project requires. Setting up a three-level keyword-based system test automation involves a significant investment in time and resources and is often surplus to requirements for small-scale or short-term projects. There are, however, tools available that simplify the setup of test architectures (see [URL: Testtoolreview]). *Keyword-based system test automation has high startup costs.*

Test automation setup tasks can also be decoupled from tasks that are directly connected with product development. Product development involves implementing features and writing the corresponding system tests in keyword notation. If the test sequence control mechanism is already available, keyword-based tests can be run immediately—however, if sequence control is not yet ready, some of the tests may run automatically while the rest will temporarily have to be run manually, even though the things the tester should test manually are defined in the keyword notation.

Little or no knowledge of the product's specific logic is required to program the sequence control mechanism. Test automation know-how is much more important. Writing the application, drafting the system tests (in keyword notation) and programming the test sequence controller are therefore tasks that can be distributed among the members of the team, and Sprint Planning can be used to ensure that the development of each keeps pace with that of the others. Developing a test sequence controller from scratch of course requires more effort and thus needs to be given a high priority within the first few Sprints.

6.4.3   Behavior-Driven Testing

Another way to draft and automate tests using a domain specific language (DSL) is to use behavior-driven testing (BDT) techniques (see [URL: BDT]). This approach uses a more natural language than the keyword and table-based approach detailed above.

However, the two approaches overlap and it is quite possible to save the keywords you have already defined in a central, hierarchical repository and use then to specify BDT test scripts.

There are a number of BDT frameworks available (such as Fit, FitNesse, Cucumber, JBehave, Specs2 and Behat (see [URL: Testtoolreview])) that support the automation of BDT test cases. Automation takes place using a similar approach to that taken by keyword-driven testing, in that a feature is tested using various scenarios. A scenario corresponds to a test case and is divided into sections according to the principle of `Given-When-Then`, which correspond largely to the `setup-procedure-check` sections of a unit test case (see section 4.1.2).

The eHome team selects the PHP-compatible framework, Behat, and uses it to create the following test script:

Case Study 6–6

eHome Controller Case Study 6-6: System test case drafted as a behavior-driven test using Behat

Feature: `device_control`
As an eHome owner, I want to control various classes of device (e.g., lamps, dimmers, blinds) but, in order to avoid faulty operation, the controller only allows commands for each class of device to be executed by that device.

Scenario: Switch lamp on and off
 Given device "lamp" in "kitchen" at "window"
 When switch "on" "lamp" in "kitchen" at "window"
 Then status "lamp" in "kitchen" at "window" is "on"

The team has to implement the keywords and parameters that occur in the scenario (e.g., `switch` and `"lamp"`) in corresponding test scripts. For example, the switch command has to be programmed as a PHP function that follows the following pattern:

```
/**
 * @When /^switch "([^"]*)" "([^"]*)" in "([^"]*)" at "([^"]*)"$/
 */

public function switchInAt($arg1, $arg2, $arg3, $arg4) {

    ...
}
```

When the test is performed, Behat calls the PHP function using the following parameters:

```
switchInAt("on", "lamp", "kitchen", "window");;
```

Using a BDT framework also creates a multi-layer test architecture (see fig. 6-1). Like unit test frameworks, BDT frameworks also use the test object's API as the test automation interface. If this API is located on a higher test architecture level, BDT can partially replace system test cases that would otherwise have to be performed through the product's user interface.

Unit test cases (see chapter 4) can be drafted using BDT too, although the effort required to find the right wording is seldom justified. Compared with a system-level requirement, the API of a single class usually only implements partial or basic functionality that is simpler to express in terms of API methods and their parameters than it is in terms of system requirements. If, however, you wish your unit or integration test cases to be intelligible to people who don't understand program code or conventional test code, BDT can be a useful tool to use.

BDT and API tests

6.5 Using Test First for System Testing

Test First means writing and automating one or more test cases before the code that is to be tested is written or edited[5]. If these tests are passed without revealing any defects, this is seen as a done criterion for the corresponding programming task. This approach works very well in the context of unit and integration testing (see chapters 4 and 5), but can it be applied to system testing too?

Because GUI test tools require direct access to the application's user interface, if the tests in question are recorded or coded using a GUI test tool, the test object and its user interface have to exist. The principles of Test First cannot be applied in this context.

Keyword-based system test cases

If system test cases are drafted using keyword-based or BDT techniques (i.e., using vocabulary based on business logic), the result will be test cases that function independently of the technical implementation of the product and its user interface. Such test cases can therefore also be drafted before the test object exists. Keyword-based and BDT techniques are therefore not just helpful when it comes to modularizing test automation tasks but can also be used to implement Test First techniques on a system testing level.

6.5.1 System Test Repository

For the team to work successfully using keyword-based testing or BDT (and thereby Test First too), it has to agree on the vocabulary and notation that are to be used. If new keywords are introduced in an uncontrolled way, you run the risk of re-inventing keywords that address system features that are already covered by existing keywords. In turn, this leads to the creation of redundant test cases or multiple versions of current tests. It is therefore essential to build up a central dictionary where the team collects and manages its keywords.

Test*Bench* (see [URL: Testtoolreview]) is a great tool for doing just that. The team can use its repository to store keywords using standardized notation and new test cases can be built from combinations of keywords via drag and drop. Reference lists show which keywords and parameters are used in which cases and can be used to monitor changes to keywords or test cases. The tool significantly reduces the amount of effort involved in managing changes to the system test suite.

---

5.   "Write a failing automated test before changing any code" [Beck/Andres 04, chapter 7].

6.5.2   Pair Programming

Pair programming is a useful additional technique that will help you to stick to Test First principles while system testing. Different pairs can be used to address different types of tasks:

Drafting new system test cases
Before coding begins, the programmer needs to draft the required test cases. Especially in the case of system tests, this should always be done in a pair with a tester, who can make sure that the system test cases view the system from a user's perspective and cover all the specified requirements. In the meantime, the programmer can help the tester to focus on writing tests exclusively aimed at the feature in question.

Drafting and maintaining keywords
Specialist knowledge of the application and its domain are the most important skills when it comes to naming relevant keywords (and their parameters) and entering the corresponding definitions into the repository. This task can often be performed by a single tester. However, building and maintaining a well-conceived library of keywords throughout all the Sprints in a project is much harder to do, and experience has shown that pairs of testers produce better results and work more efficiently than a single tester working alone.

Automating keywords
This task is all about implementing keywords using test scripts on all tiers of the test sequence controller. This requires programming using the GUI test tool's scripting language and can involve programming in xUnit or other scripting languages. This task is best performed by teams made up of testers and programmers.

6.6   Non-functional Testing

The system tests that we have detailed so far are all functional system tests that check whether the software fulfills its functional requirements—i.e., whether issuing a command such as "switch lamp on" actually executes the appropriate action.

Software products are also subject to a large number of non-func-   *ISO 25010*
tional requirements. According to [Spillner/Linz 14, chapter 3], "Non-functional requirements describe attributes of a system's functional behavior—in other words, how well and at what level of quality a (sub-)

system performs its intended task. The implementation of non-functional requirements has a significant influence on customer satisfaction and the degree to which the end-user enjoys using the product." The attributes in question are performance efficiency, compatibility, usability, reliability, security[6], maintainability and portability, and are described in detail in [ISO 25010][7]. The fulfillment of non-functional requirements has to be checked using appropriate tests. According to [Spillner/Linz 14][8] these include:

- **Load testing**
  Measuring system behavior with increasing load—for example, with increasing numbers of parallel users or database transactions.

- **Performance testing**
  Measuring the processing speed and response time for specific use cases, usually under increasing load.

- **Volume testing/Mass testing/Stress testing**
  Observation of system behavior for varying amounts of data (for example, when processing very large files) and when overloaded.

- **Security testing** against unauthorized system or data access.

- **Reliability** and **stability testing** under continuous use (for example, measuring how many system failures occur per hour for a particular usage profile).

- **Compatibility and data conversion testing**
  Checking interoperability with existing systems and data import/export processes.

- **Robustness testing** in case of misuse, programming errors, hardware failure, etc., and testing of error handling and recovery.

- **Configuration testing** for various different system configurations—for example, using different version of the operating system, different languages or varying hardware platforms.

---

6.   The "safety" aspect of system behavior in case of system misuse or failure should not be confused with "security."

7.   ISO 25010:2011 is part of the set of standards "Software Engineering—Software Product Quality Requirements and Evaluation (SquaRE)" and, in 2011, replaced Part 1 of the previous quality standard [ISO 9126].

8.   [Crispin/Gregory 08] classifies software testing using a four-quadrant scheme. Non-functional tests belong to quadrant #4, which covers "technology oriented, automatable tests." Usability tests are seen as manual tests that belong to quadrant #3.

Usability
Checking how easy the system is to learn and use. Includes checking the intelligibility of system output depending on the needs of various user groups (see also [ISO 9241]).

Documentation checks
Checking that the content of the documentation (user manuals, training materials, etc.) matches system behavior.

Changeability and maintainability
Checking the accuracy and up-to-dateness of the development documents, sytem structure, etc.

Checking and testing these requirements presents an agile team with a number of challenges:

- Load, performance, volume and other, similar tests are, by definition, extensive and long-term. If they are embedded in the CI process, they can slow it down significantly, and are often too protracted for inclusion in the nightly build process.
- Robustness, hardware failure, recovery and other, similar tests are difficult to automate and usually require manual intervention during setup and testing of the test environment.
- User-friendliness testing, documentation checks and code maintainability tests require manual intervention and extensive reviews.

Non-functional requirements have to be addressed early in the project and require continual review and testing. The most obvious solution is to package all these tests in a single system test Sprint. However, this strategy (see section 6.8.1) has a serious drawback, namely: feedback is not provided in a timely fashion. With relation to non-functional requirements, this represents a great risk, as negative attributes such as poor performance or usability are usually caused by fundamental system architecture or design defects that cannot be rectified by rewriting a line or two of code. When these types of defects are discovered, comprehensive refactoring is often required.

There are various ways the team can address this dilemma:

- Long-term testing: The features that are to be created or modified during the current Sprint are defined during the Sprint Planning phase, as are the corresponding acceptance criteria. These include all non-functional requirements that are affected or required locally by the feature(s) in question. The design and (if possible) automation of appropriate tests that check non-functional attributes in a feature-oriented fashion are an essential part of the task list and have to be carried out during the Sprint. To do this, the Scrum Master needs to go through the above checklist of non-functional attributes with the team to decide which are relevant to the feature in question. The resulting tests then have to be performed at least once during the Sprint. This approach ensures that, at the end of the Sprint, the team receives usable feedback regarding the non-functional aspects of any new features and whether any architectural issues exist that can be addressed in the next Sprint.
- Robustness, hardware failure and other, similar tests can be performed as exploratory tests, although full regression analysis for all robustness tests is not usually necessary. Instead, a limited number of robustness tests are selected from a list and are added to the Sprint task list.
- User-friendliness, documentation, code maintainability and other, similar tests are conducted continuously from an early stage using the pair programming approach. Instead of conducting comprehensive time-consuming reviews at the end of the Sprint (or in a separate system test Sprint), the appropriate checks are performed on a daily (or continuous) basis by the paired teams. To ensure test reliability, the Scrum Master issues a list of relevant testing aspects to each pair and periodically checks each team's findings and countermeasures. Non-functional attributes are seldom local attributes of a single feature and are more usually global system (or system architecture) attributes, so it is essential that the Scrum Master holds regular reviews to discuss test results with the team. Regardless of the overall picture, the team then has to decide, for example, which tasks that address improving use-friendliness should be included in the Product Backlog or the next Sprint Backlog.

The checking and testing of non-functional requirements is hampered by the fact that they are often imprecisely defined. Requirements such as "The systems must be easy to use" or "The system should react quickly" are not testable and therefore cannot be used as acceptance criteria. If it uses Test First, an agile team will have a large pool of functional tests that it can use to define and test non-functional system attributes, making this aspect of project management much easier.

"Scenarios are selected from the existing functional tests that represent a cross-section of the system's overall functionality, whereby each non-functional aspect that is to be tested has to be observable within the chosen test scenario. During testing, the non-functional factor is measured against a predefined threshold value and is deemed to have passed the test if the value is upheld. In other words, the functional test scenario serves as a measuring instruction that tests the selected non-functional attribute" [Spillner/Linz 14, chapter 3]. This way, the selected test cases serve not only as test instructions, but also help define requirements and document system behavior.

6.7   Automated Acceptance Testing

The Product Owner is not limited to using system tests when preparing acceptance tests. Automated unit or integration test cases can also contribute usefully to an acceptance test suite, and the Product Owner can use automated system tests instead of testing manually.

The acceptance criteria that have to be fulfilled are the critical factor when it comes to deciding which tests to use, and have to be addressed using a suitable subset of the available automated tests. Acceptance tests only have to be performed manually for criteria that are not yet covered by existing automated tests.

Case Study 6–7

eHome Controller Case Study 6-7: Conformance test suite

eHome Tools licenses its product to a partner who also manufactures home automation devices that are to be equipped with the eHome Controller software. Of course, the licensor requires the software to work seamlessly with his/her products, so a comprehensive automated conformance test suite is an important part of the approval and certification process the product has to go through.

eHome Tools includes the conformance test suite in the integration testing phase of its CI process, thus guaranteeing conformance and customer acceptance for all future updates.

6.8   When Should System Testing Take Place?

In agile projects, system testing is usually much less automated than unit and integration testing[9]. System testing usually involves a fair amount of manual intervention that can take a number of days to complete. Because each Sprint generates new features that require their own system tests, the number of manual system tests grows from Sprint to Sprint.

Even after just a few Sprints it becomes clear that the team cannot perform all its system tests for every Sprint the way it does for its unit and integration tests, and even less so for every change in the code. The team then has to carefully plan when to perform which system tests. The following sections describe a number of approaches to system test timing.

6.8.1   System Testing in a Final Sprint

Fig. 6–2
System testing in a final Sprint

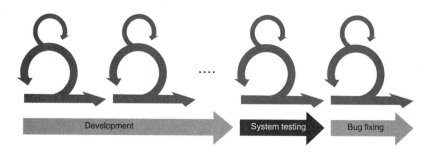

This is the simplest system test timing strategy, and involves planning a separate "system test Sprint." This approach is easy to plan and can be used for exclusively manual system tests. The system test Sprint contains only system testing tasks. The drawbacks of this approach are:

▨ You can only tell if you have a potentially shippable product once the system test Sprint has been completed. If the system test Sprint is still pending, shipping a product involves a high level of risk.
▨ The amount of bug fixing and retesting effort involved can only be estimated once the system test Sprint is complete, and can involve additional bug-fix or retest Sprints.

---

9.   In traditionally managed projects, these proportions are usually reversed. The independently organized system testing group builds a comprehensive, automated GUI test system, while programmers who have little QA and testing experience are only marginally involved in creating unit tests.

░ System testing feedback to the developer only takes place after the final system test Sprint, which is often much too late. The aim of providing timely feedback to the programmers is not met.

The overall procedure is very similar to traditional V-model system testing and falls short of utilizing the advantages of agile practices—especially the creation of a potentially shippable product after every Sprint.

One way to work around these disadvantages is to form an independent system testing team. (Case study 8.5, "Scrum in a Medical Technology Environment," describes a good example of this approach). The new team can shoulder the system test Sprint while the product team has more capacity to push ahead with the next development-related Sprint. This way, development and system testing can run in parallel at a one-Sprint offset. Bugs that are discovered in the course of a System test Sprint can be debugged during the next development Sprint and, from a programmer's point of view, the feedback loop is only two Sprints long.

Independent system testing team

6.8.2   System Testing at the End of a Sprint

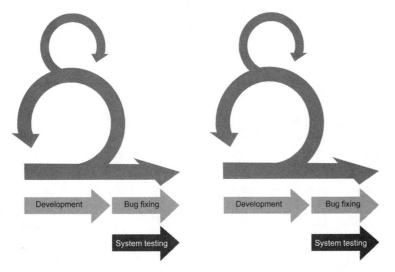

Fig. 6–3
System testing
at the end of a Sprint

This strategy involves performing system testing in a specially reserved slot at the end of each Sprint, and is suitable for use in simpler projects that do not require a lot of system testing. If the amount of system testing effort threatens to expand too far, the team has to select which system tests to perform and which to leave out of each Sprint. In this case, it is important for the test manager to keep an eye on the situation, which an increasing degree of system test automation will help to improve. The disadvantages of this strategy are:

- As with the system test Sprint strategy, this approach also produces an unknown quantity of bug fixing and retesting tasks at the end of the Sprint, thus endangering the planned timebox.
- To gain time for bug fixing tasks while sticking to the planned timebox, User Stories have to be regularly removed from the Sprint Backlog.
- Because time is limited and only selected system tests can be performed, the risk of overlooking defects and carrying them over into subsequent Sprints increases. This risk is less severe if you perform regression testing for all system test cases.
- A programmer has to wait until the end of the Sprint to receive feedback. If the corresponding system test cases are included in the done criteria for a programming task (as it should be), these tasks remain "undone" until the end of the Sprint, making it impossible to effectively estimate project velocity.

Sprints become serialized like a waterfall. Feedback to the team takes place within the Sprint although the tasks are serialized like a waterfall. Because system testing always reveals some defects, a certain amount of time has to be reserved for bug fixes and retesting. The Sprint is therefore inevitably divided into programming, system testing, and bug-fixing phases—a situation often referred to as a "Water-Scrum-Fall."

6.8.3   System Testing Nonstop

The system testing nonstop strategy applies the principles of unit and integration testing to system testing, and is probably the best solution. "System testing nonstop" means automating system tests as far as possible and integrating them in the automated CI process like unit and integration tests. According to the required preconditions and run times, system test cases can be grouped into suites that can be run or hidden, and the resulting CI environment includes all the project's tests, from unit to system level.

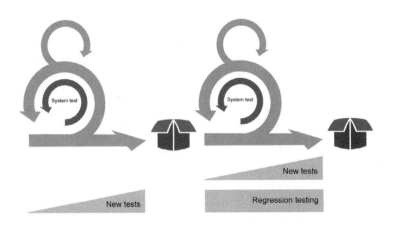

Fig. 6–4
System testing nonstop

Because of the amount of time required to run integration and system tests, not all test cases are performed during each CI run. However, the team has the option to choose a suitable mixture of unit, integration and system tests before starting the CI process. Full testing can still take place during the nightly build, giving the team full feedback (including system test feedback) at least once a day. Case study 8.2 provides an example of system testing nonstop in practice.

Nightly build

If system tests for a new feature are to be run in the first nightly build, system tests have to be automated in parallel with the development of new features. This is the only way to ensure that the team gets regular, daily system feedback.

System testing nonstop assumes that system testing has been thoroughly automated, and using Test First principles for system testing is a great way to help the process along (see also section 6.5: Using Test First for System Testing).

6.9   The Release Sprint and Deployment

If Continuous Integration is implemented well, a Sprint will produce several completely tested builds. Contrary to many people's expectations, the final build isn't always the shippable result of the Sprint, and the Product Owner decides which build should become the release candidate. Later builds are not always better than earlier ones and can, for instance lack a finished GUI or be less stable than earlier versions. The team can remove a feature from the Sprint Backlog if it takes up too much time and either leave it out entirely or finish the Sprint with a build that doesn't include it.

With the team's support, the Product Owner takes the decision regarding which build to release toward the end of the Sprint, and the chosen candidate is not developed any further. Any remaining time can then be used to complete the documentation and finish any pending manual tests. These usually take the form of exploratory or session-based tests (see also section 6.3: Manual System Testing). Any bug fixing that is required takes place in parallel. The weighting of the tasks that take place toward the end of a Sprint thus shifts from developing and testing new features to testing and bug fixing.

Internal and external releases   Release candidates are not necessarily released into the wild. Scrum Teams that produce monthly release candidates often only approve and release the product itself every three or six months. This is because releases that are implemented outside of the team environment generate additional work, especially for the support, marketing and sales departments, who all have to bring their systems and activities up to date when a new release appears. These activities have to be accounted for in a company's internal workflow when introducing Scrum product development methodology and when deciding how often to produce new releases. Too many releases are not always good for the customer either, as each new version takes time to implement and produces extra costs (not just in the IT department).

Once the decision has been taken to deliver a new release, the complete product (including software, manuals, tutorials, etc.) has to be put together. These processes too, can be largely automated within a Scrum Team. All the required files are taken from the configuration management system and packaged using scripts. The complete package is then transferred to a server where it can be downloaded or burned to DVD.

Continuous Deployment   If the deployment process has been automated, it can be included in the project's CI environment, giving the team Continuous Deployment capability. Provided that all tests pass, this means that every change in the code produces not only a new build, but also a new version of the product that includes the code, the required configuration files and corresponding documentation.

Because not all test cases are always run and the production of user documentation cannot be fully automated, not every build run will result in deployment. However, daily deployment is nevertheless a realistic target, especially in Web development environments where the system testing environment and the target environment hardly differ, and the online target environment is directly accessible from the CI environment. Under such conditions, the product can be uploaded and automatically installed on an external Web server as the last step in the CI run.

6.10 System Test Management

System testing presents a Scrum Team with multiple challenges. These begin with the decision as to when to write and run system tests, progress through setting up the test environment and the automation Architecture. The final question is which tests to perform as unit, integration, and system tests. In a traditional V-model project, a separate testing team operating at full capacity is dedicated to tackling all these tasks. In a Scrum Team, you shouldn't simply assume that the team will be able to deal with system testing along with all the other tasks that it is already busy with.

System testing tasks have to be actively addressed during Sprint Planning, and part of the team's capacity has to be explicitly allocated to system testing. Ideally, the team will keep an eye on all aspects of system test management but, if this is not the case, it is the Scrum Master's job to solve the issue—for example, by electing a tester to the role of test manager. The test manager's job is to make sure the team is up to facing the challenges listed above and to judge the quality of the tests the team creates. This involves periodically reviewing individual tests and test results with a view to creating new tests or rewriting old ones where necessary. The test manager also has to help the Product Owner to interpret test results and judge product quality.

Include system testing tasks in Sprint Planning

All members of the team should take a look at the results of the tests performed during the nightly build, but it is the test manager's job to interpret the results and define the resulting team activities.

The basic Scrum rules state that every defect has to be remedied immediately by the programmer, although it is still preferable if all new bugs are roughly analyzed before the Daily Standup. The team then discusses any new issues and, if necessary, creates new tasks for any problems that are obviously too serious to be addressed any other way. Bugs that require their own, new tasks also have to be entered in the defect management system or appropriately flagged within the task.

Daily bug analysis before the Daily Standup

If the team uses a system-test Sprint or Water-Scrum-Fall strategy (see above), the test manager has to select a range of tests that can be performed within the allotted system testing timeframe. If these include manual tests, the test manager also has to decide which are to be run as regression tests on a daily or weekly basis. The greater the proportion of manual tests, the more similar the agile testing process will become to traditional test management. If this is the case in your project, you will need to take particular care to select the required tests based on risk assessment and to keep a careful eye on the results they produce when distributed among the team.

It would be naive to assume that manual tests don't need to be monitored just because the people performing them are working in an agile team. Agile practices mean that every team member has innumerable tasks to attend to that are much more interesting than repeating a manual test. Pair programming, predefined tests and checklists for each pair, and Daily Scrums ensure that testing is as effective as possible, and the test manager can always intervene if necessary.

Build your test framework step by step

The drudgery of manual testing is a good incentive to work on your project's test automation. As we have seen, test frameworks can be very elegant, but the more complex they are, the greater the risk that the team spends more time optimizing the framework than it does drafting and running the required test cases. Just like when you are developing a product, when you are developing a testing framework, you should build up your framework step by step and only include the components that you really need right now. Over-the-top, up-front framework development doesn't help at all.

6.11 Questions and Exercises

6.11.1 Self-Assessment

Questions and exercises to help you assess how agile your project or team really is.

1. Does the team differentiate between unit, integration and system tests?
2. How many test cases do we have on each of the three levels? How highly automated are they? Which (and how many) test cases are embedded in the CI system?
3. Do we have multiple test environments?
4. When does the team perform system tests? In a separate system test Sprint, at the end of the Sprint, or nonstop?
5. How do we automate our system tests? Using recorded GUI tests (record/playback) or using scripts?

6. If we use scripts, which approach does the team use? Keywords? DSL? BDT?

7. When do we write our system test cases? Using Test First before we implement a feature? Or later when the feature is part of a running build?

8. Which non-functional tests do we have? Do they cover all the types of tests listed in ISO 25010?

9. Do we differentiate between system tests and acceptance tests?

10. Who decides which build becomes a release candidate?

11. When do we build an external release? Do we have a predefined release schedule?

12. How is the role of test manager filled within the team? Do we have an explicit or implicit dedicated test manager? Or has the role been neglected?

6.11.2 Methods and Techniques

These questions will help you to review the content of the current chapter.

1. Explain the relationships between the Product Backlog, acceptance criteria and system test cases.

2. Explain the term "end-to-end testing."

3. What are the basic requirements of a system testing environment? What are the differences between system and unit testing?

4. Explain exploratory and session-based testing.

5. What is an acceptance test?

6. Explain the drawbacks of record/playback-based test automation.

7. How does a keyword-driven test work?

8. Explain how a multi-level test architecture works. What are its major advantages and disadvantages?

9. Explain the basic ways to plan the timing of system testing within a Scrum project and list the advantages and disadvantages of each.

6.11.3 Other Exercises

These exercises will help you delve deeper into topics touched on in the course of the chapter.

1. With reference to figure 3-2 on page 31, which interfaces in the eHome architecture diagram are used in the eHome system test examples described in this chapter?

2. Draft keyword-based system test cases for the "Switch Programming" Backlog entry in section 3.3 using the corresponding acceptance criteria listed in exercise 3.9.3-2.

3. Draft the same test cases as data-driven tests and enter the corresponding test data in a table.

4. Which additional test cases do we need if the program's auto-repeat function can be defined using a relative term such as "+2 hours." Use Test First to define the desired program behavior.

7 Quality Management and Quality Assurance

Traditional quality management (QM) is heavily document-driven, whereas agile practices require documentation to be reduced to a minimum. What effects does this have on the work of a quality manager or QA department? How can QA specialists use their know-how to contribute to the success of an agile team? What is the best way to deal with regulatory requirements and external audits? This chapter provides the answers to all these questions.

7.1 Traditional Quality Management

7.1.1 The ISO 9000 Standard

A quality management (QM) system is made up of the accountability and process rules a company works to, the documentation of these rules (process descriptions, procedural and work instructions, best practices and guidelines), and mechanisms designed to monitor and continually improve the QM system itself. The operative activities that apply these rules and check that the quality requirements for a product are upheld are referred to as quality assurance, or QA (see section 7.4).

QM system documentation includes a visualization of the responsibilities and all business processes that are relevant to meeting the company's quality objectives. These usually include development/engineering, procurement/purchasing, production and maintenance/service, and regulating all quality assurance procedures that take place within these processes as well as the overall quality management system, with all its quality policies, quality targets, responsibilities and optimization processes.

Visualizing business processes

Most large organizations adhere to the quality management guidelines laid out in the [ISO 9000] family of standards. [ISO 9001] defines the minimum requirements of a QM system and lists the topics for which rules

ISO 9000

exist and need to be documented. These standards developed from the QA concepts used by manufacturing industries. The 1994 version of ISO 9001 defines 20 basic elements of quality management that reflect the processes involved in manufacturing, from development and engineering through production and control of nonconforming products, right up to assembly and customer service. A broad-based interpretation of these elements was necessary when they were used to represent the processes employed by service industries and software development companies. ISO 9001:2000 was a more process-oriented version of the standard and differentiates between management processes (i.e., decision-making and legal roles), value creation (development, production, services and maintenance) and (internal) support processes such as accounting, procurement/purchasing, and supply chain management. A QM system has to cover the responsibilities and processes that govern all these activities.

The category that software development is assigned to depends on its importance within a company. A software development company will most likely assign its main activity to value creation, while a trading company is more likely to see it as a support process that ensures that its IT systems are reliably maintained. Centralized configuration management, QM/QA activities, and personnel management are usually classed as support processes too.

7.1.2 The Principles of PDCA

An ISO 9000 QM system is based on the PDCA cycle [ISO 9001, section 0.2], also known as the Deming cycle [URL: PDCA]:

- Plan: The process is planned (i.e., defined) with regard to aims, the steps involved, responsibilities, prerequisites, resources and desired results.
- Do: The predefined process is put into practice and the expected results or planned product ensues.
- Check: The results of the process are compared with the predefined requirements and the results of these checks are reported.
- Act: Corrective actions on significant differences between the actual and planned results are requested with a view to continual quality improvement.

PDCA cycles can be performed at various levels within an organization:

The PDCA cycle at various levels

■ **Operative level**
A running process or activity is run (routinely) according to pre-defined guidelines. The results are produced, checked, corrected if necessary, and delivered.

■ **Management level**
A process is reworked or completely redefined (for example, during a company reorganization) and is implemented, perhaps as part of a pilot project. The effectiveness and acceptability of the process are monitored and, if necessary, adjusted and optimized. Certification for use outside of the pilot project follows.

■ **QM system level**
The effectiveness of every predefined QM process is checked regularly using data provided by reference values, status reports, internal or external audits, and other tools such as a company suggestion box or customer feedback. Processes that are found to be deficient are reworked and improved. The PDCA cycle thus generates a continuous top-down quality improvement process.

7.1.3   Strengths and Weaknesses

ISO 9000-based quality management has proved to be highly successful. It supports company-wide standardization, motivates those involved to clarify and stick to their responsibilities, and makes a company more transparent to its staff and customers. If required, it also provides a built-in audit interface that makes it easy for third parties to attain a detailed overview of how the company works. This can be used to build up trust but also to exert pressure.

The drawbacks of ISO 9000-based quality management are[1]:

■ **Its extent**
ISO 9000 requires QM-related business processes to be described (i.e., specified) as part of the QM documentation. The extent of QM documentation depends on the size of the organization, the type of work it is engaged in, the complexity of the processes involved and the competence of the staff who execute it [see ISO 9001, section 4.2.1]. Processes

---

1.   Some of these were detailed in a project management context in Chapter 2.

are, however, often described in too much detail, which can help people who are not familiar with the operative aspects of a process to understand and/or carry it out without further instruction. Additionally, process audits have to be capable of proving that a process is carried out according to its description, which can lead to the production of process logs and other records that do not contribute directly to value creation and only serve to prove to (internal) auditors that the process is carried out correctly. All this can result in a huge set of QM documents made up of the QM manual, a description of each process, various guidelines for customizing the process descriptions to fit project constraints, templates, template fill-in help, etc.

Resistance to change

Changing or updating the content of individual process steps can be quite time-consuming. Modification of a step can necessitate changes in other places within the document hierarchy, which then has to be brought completely up to date. Additionally, QM systems are usually valid for the entire company, so making changes involves reaching agreements with many individuals and groups spread around the organization, which can be a disincentive to making changes. Even if you have found enough supporters for a change and you have agreed on the changes to the content this involves, any alterations still have to successfully pass formal approval procedures. To avoid having to make all this effort, necessary changes are often ignored or postponed.

Not necessarily current

If the documentation is not updated sufficiently often, real-world processes will sooner or later diverge from their written counterparts, making the provision of documentary proof of process problematic. Because the real-world process runs differently from the way it is described, it cannot be shown to conform to the QM guidelines and will produce discrepancies during the next audit.

Risk of a parallel system

To avoid audit discrepancies, it is tempting to produce the logs required by the QM system in a pro forma fashion. If this is allowed to take place, the company will quickly end up with a QM system on paper that has little to do with the processes that are executed in the real world. If a QM system is too theoretical or if its rules are not adequately adopted (or meet with too little acceptance), this too can lead to discrepancies between theory and reality that make it impossible to achieve the system's aims.

7.1.4   Process Modeling and Software Development

When software development processes are defined using a QM system, this emphasizes the complexity of the process and the difficulties involved in modeling it. It is extremely difficult—or impossible—to formally differentiate between individual phases or steps.

Even if the process is only defined in the form of roughly outlined phases, it is difficult enough to define criteria that accurately describe the beginning, end, or results of these phases (see section 2.3, fig. 2-3). The question of whether a particular milestone has been reached is a matter of interpretation. Creating a more precise definition of the process doesn't help either, and only serves to create increasing numbers of special cases, exceptions and document templates. In other words, it is impossible to come to a formal conclusion regarding whether a development step defined in the model has been productively and correctly completed. This is not only because software development is a non-deterministic, empirical process, but also because the sequence of intermediate products (requirements, rough specifications, fine specifications, code) produced by the process cannot be formally mapped to one another, however hard software development methods or information technology tools attempt to do so.

Let's take a look at an example. Assuming we want to distinguish between the rough and fine specification phases of a product in the process model, the QM department could draft two sample templates using arbitrarily chosen structures and boundaries between the two phases. However, this approach does not guarantee that a correctly filled out fine specification describes the planned product more accurately or realistically than a correctly filled out rough specification. The project team could simply leave out the rough specification but still create a usable fine specification or even begin coding without using any specifications at all (although the latter approach is unlikely to result in an acceptable product). On the other hand, it is also possible for the team to completely miss its target if it works according to templates that are comprehensive but filled with weak content.

The only way to satisfactorily solve this problem is to agree in advance on the desired results of each phase and to check and review each one. In this case, a detailed process description is no more help than a roughly drafted, keyword-based phase model.

7.2   Agile Quality Management

The weaknesses of conventional QM systems listed in the previous section make it clear why some agile teams, purists and gurus reject process documentation and QM systems outright. Such a dogmatic approach often leads to the other extreme, creating projects or teams with no written rules. The company's usual procedures are rejected on the grounds of their being not agile; but new, better rules are not created to replace them because documentation is regarded as unproductive waste. In some cases, the waste argument is a useful justification for ignoring the usual rules and not producing any product or QA documentation.

Agile software development processes require documentation too.

Even if it is not popular with some team members, agile software development processes also require documentation in order to be adequately defined. If interpreted correctly, agile methodology does not reject rules outright—agile teams need rules too! However, any rules have to serve the team and not vice versa[2], and it is always better to stick to a few rules than to completely ignore a complex system of rules that only exists on paper. A QM system designed to support the principles of the Agile Manifesto [URL: Agile Manifesto] and find favor with agile teams has to be lean. In other words, it has to be simple, easy to maintain and always up to date.

If a company already uses an ISO 9000-based QM system (which will usually be the case), the agile software development process can be added to the existing documentation in the form of an additional process. The degree to which the agile teams accept this approach will depend on the degree to which the existing QM system suffers from the shortcomings listed in section 7.1.3. It usually makes more sense to introduce an extensive realignment of the existing documentation and QM culture.

7.2.1   Simplifying QM Documentation

The team has to clearly state which agile methodology it is using (Scrum, Kanban, or others) but doesn't need to describe this in detail. It is sufficient to name the methods, techniques and measures that are used and to out-

---

2.   The Agile Manifesto says, "Individuals and interactions over processes and tools" [URL: Agile Manifesto].

line how they are implemented on a company or team level. These should include the form, location and prioritization of the Backlog, the type and frequency of meetings, the basic shape of the CI process, the principles of Test First, and the location of saved test cases, etc. Details of all these can be referred to in the corresponding literature, the manuals of the tools being used and, of course, in the artifacts produced by the project itself.

Instead of drafting a complex process model, a simple diagram like the one shown in fig. 2-1 is sufficient to illustrate the basic form of a project. Instead of detailing a complex array of processes and process steps, this illustration shows the required tools, such as the Backlog, the Daily Scrum, the Definition of Done, etc. The "how" of the project is a natural result of applying techniques such as Backlog Refinement, Planning Poker, Test First, etc. Because they are prerequisites of the methodology, the process description doesn't have to separately describe these techniques. All in all, the process description is reduced to a length of just a few pages.

Don't forget to train staff in the appropriate techniques! Just because the QM system implicitly requires appropriate know-how, this doesn't mean that the team members involved are actually up to speed on the required methodology. On-the-job training and advanced training plans have to include literature, training, coaching and off-site conferences for each of the techniques used by the team.

Techniques have to be taught.

Agile teams often describe the rules they work by in a self-penned Team Charter (see section 3.6). This document is only valid within the team. A Team Charter is usually quite concise and therefore makes a good starting point for a description of the agile development process in the QM system. However, because the QM system documentation is aimed at a larger set of readers (other teams, management, external auditors and even the customer), the language and special know-how included in the Charter will usually have to be rewritten before it is adopted as part of the QM documentation.

If multiple Scrum Teams are working on a project, the development process has to be described in a general form so that it is valid for all the teams, while the precise definition remains the job of each team. The task board is a typical example of just such a point. The QM system (or the company-wide agile process) will usually demand that each team has its own task board. However, whether it is kept electronically or in the form of a magnet board (or whatever) is up to the team. The Team Charter is the document in which each team-specific implementation is logged.

The Team Charter documents a team-specific implementation.

While integrating agile methodology into the QM system, you have to decide which of the existing QM practices (project planning requirements, required metrics, test result documentation, development tools used, etc.) should be perpetuated in the new, agile environment. If all the existing practices are thrown overboard, you risk making the entire QM system obsolete, but if all existing standards are kept, the QM system will hinder the agile approach or even make it (formally) impossible to implement. Appropriate rules (for example, regarding the tools to be used) should therefore be formulated as recommendations. Agile principles leave establishing the form of the development process to the team. Neither QM staff nor the Scrum Master can give the team unilateral instructions, and are there only to advise and makes recommendations.

This process of change is not just about updating documentation, but also about the recognition and acceptance of agile practices by the organization. And, in places where external compliance requirements have to be fulfilled (see section 7.3), you have to make it clear to agile teams that a QM system and a few non-agile rules nevertheless have to be adhered to.

7.2.2 Changing QM Culture

Conventional quality management is a top-down process. A central QM team[3] is responsible for documenting and, where it makes sense, standardizing the processes involved. The team drafts the process manuals and rolls out standardized processes in all relevant departments. In contrast, agile methodology is a bottom-up process. Agile teams devise their own working methods, so QM staff have to learn to adapt.

A team that is accustomed to unifying processes has to transform itself into a group that helps teams to document their own self-penned processes. This way, a central, standard-setting unit becomes a group that encourages the exchange of information between teams and publicizes methods that work well. The QM team also has to suggest alternatives for working methods that don't function as planned.

The QM team becomes a service group.   The QM team becomes a mentor and a group that provides a service. Agile teams are seen as customers who can request the group's services. If,

---

3. In small and medium-sized companies, this will usually be a dedicated member of staff and a number of ancillary workers, while large organizations (and safety-related production units) usually have a separate QM department. To keep things simple, all these various forms will be referred to as QM staff or QM team in the course of this chapter.

for example, a team wishes to improve its CI process by introducing a new CI tool it can request that the QM team looks for a tool that fits the team's requirements and implements it. In the meantime, the development team can concentrate on its day-to-day work. This way, process optimization is initiated by the development team but its implementation is delegated to the QM team.

If a QM team has to serve multiple agile teams, it has to balance its activities to support the interests of the various teams with regard to each other and within the context of the entire organization. However, it is still the development teams themselves who decide which of the QM team's recommendations to accept, even if this means that a planned standardization cannot be completely adopted. The QM team has to face this acceptance test and, if one of its recommendations is rejected, needs to consider why and what it could do to improve the situation.

The QM team should use the opportunity to organize itself as an agile team—perhaps using Kanban methodology. Working this way makes a QM team quicker, leaner and better able to deliver, and will also boost its acceptance among the agile project teams. Just like a development team, a QM team should be capable of delivering a shippable product—for example, in the form of a process description that is 100 percent acceptable to all agile teams or the seamless introduction of a fully validated tool.

QM staff as an agile team

It is no surprise that some of the tasks assigned to the QM team are similar to those of the Scrum Master. Both are responsible for ensuring that predefined rules are adhered to—the QM team by implementing ISO 9000 on a corporate level, and the Scrum Master using Scrum practices for a specific team.

The QM Team and the Scrum Master

The changes that take place when a conventional QM system is transformed into an agile QM system can reduce these differences or even make them disappear completely. The QM team provides a service to all teams while the Scrum Master has to keep an eye on the success of not just his/her team but also the entire organization—and both share the same agile QM system. This transition process can lead to the QM staff and the company's Scrum Masters being integrated into a single, cross-functional, agile QM team that encompasses all the necessary know-how to methodically and effectively support the work of Scrum Teams. This expertise covers all the standards used by the organization, process modeling tools and know-how, trained assessors and auditors, specialists, trainers for agile practices and, of course, certified Scrum Masters.

7.2.3   Retrospectives and Process Improvement

One of the central elements of the ISO 9000 standard is the demand for continual improvement, and the Sprint Retrospective (see [URL: Scrum Guide]) that is built in to Scrum methodology is an effective tool for achieving just that.

A Sprint Retrospective is a team meeting that takes place after every Sprint[4] and is used to collect the team's ideas about what it could do better as a team (not how to improve the product)[5]. The resulting suggestions are prioritized before being added to the team's Product Backlog. Any points that are seen as acute impediments can be handed over directly to the Scrum Master, who can then enter them into the Impediment Backlog. Nevertheless, the approach to suggestions for improvements and the implementation of new processes and techniques is, just like the team's day-to-day work, still governed by the team's Backlog.

Process improvement is part of the daily workflow.

Process improvement is therefore nothing special for an agile team and is part of the daily workflow. Integrating process improvement into the Sprint Planning process ensures that the team has sufficient time to get to grips with any new methods[6] and also ensures that the improvement itself is put into effect during the planned Sprint (in other words, it is dealt with now rather than when we have time). Because process improvement tasks compete with development tasks for the team's attention, the focus of process improvement will quickly be reduced to fulfilling only tasks that can be realistically implemented. This way, process improvement becomes a continual short-term exercise that doesn't take up too much of the team's time.

During the following Sprint, the team can discuss with the Scrum Master whether the implemented improvement has gained traction and check whether the improvement task's acceptance criteria have been fulfilled. If the improvement affects other teams or the global QM system, it

---

4. [URL: Scrum Guide] cites "after the Sprint Review and prior to the next Sprint Planning Meeting" as the right moment to hold a Sprint Retrospective, which usually means on a monthly basis. However, a Scrum Team can elect to do things differently—after every third Sprint might be sufficient for an experienced team. XP [Beck/Andres 04], for example, suggests a "quarterly cycle" for this type of feedback meeting.

5. The Sprint Review meeting (or Sprint Demo) is the appropriate forum for discussing how to improve the product.

6. Of course, this only works if effort estimation and Sprint Planning are given equal priority.

makes sense to involve the QM team in the discussion, thus supporting a direct exchange of information at a QM level (see section 7.2.2).

7.3   Dealing with Compliance Requirements

Most companies that develop software have to adhere to externally controlled compliance requirements. Most large organizations require their suppliers to prove that an ISO 9001-certified quality management system is in use. Manufacturers of products and electronic systems in which software plays a safety-related role have to adhere to the tenets of the IEC 61508-3 standard. The automotive, medical technology, railroad and aviation industries also have to adhere to various industry-specific standards[7]. The following sections deal with the question of whether companies that develop software using agile methodology can still adhere to these types of standards and compliance requirements.

7.3.1   Requirements of Software Development Processes

None of the standards we have mentioned require the use of a traditional software development process model such as the V-model. However, they all require that software development—as a quality-related engineering process—is well defined. This means that software development processes have to be documented so that development projects can be seen to run according to predefined rules. The introduction of agile practices as a new or additional pillar of the QM system makes this requirement easy to fulfill, and section 7.2.1 provides tips on what to look out for when doing so. Other business processes can be affected too, depending on which parts of the organization adopt agile practices.

Some standards define specific requirements for certain development activities and process steps (such as the definition of safety classes in IEC [IEC 62304] and different levels of functional safety features in [ISO 26262]) combined with requirements leveled at software design and development methods such as software testing (see IEC 61508-3, section 7.4). In this case, the software development process has to include certain steps

---

7.   For example, ISO 26262 (Automotive Safety Lifecycle with Automotive Safety Integrity Level (ASIL), IEC 62304 (Medical Device—Software Life Cycle), U.S.: Food and Drug Administration (FDA) regulations, EN 50128 (Railway applications—Software for railway control and protection systems), or DO 178B (Software Considerations in Airborne Systems and Equipment Certification).

that address and reliably implement the corresponding requirements. In the examples mentioned above, a classification according to the prescribed safety levels has to take place and the resulting process has to ensure that the software artifacts are developed and checked using the level-specific guidelines thus derived.

Deriving development requirements using done criteria

Specific requirements of individual development activities can be simply derived from appropriately worded definitions of "done." If, for example, a function is to be implemented that has a high safety classification, the required test coverage is used as a done criterion for the implementation task. So far, so simple. Things get more complicated if you want to use the process to ensure that the safety classification of *every* implementation task in *every* Sprint is *always* analyzed, and impact analysis is used to define an appropriate done criterion. Checklists can help (but only if they are used conscientiously), as can selectable, preprinted task cards that contain generic done criteria (such as coverage limits). Alternatively, critical process steps that cannot be left out (such as "perform impact analysis") are represented by a separate column on the task board. How this is solved from the point of view of the process is one of the points that must be included in the QM system's process description, and which all teams have to stick to rigidly.

7.3.2 Traceability Requirements

Wherever safety-related products are developed, appropriate standards demand that design decisions and changes to the product remain reproducible and traceable even after the development process has been completed. The safety of a product[8] has to be clearly defined as part of its design attributes, functionality, and reliability implemented during the development process. Appropriate tests are then used to check that the product and its safety features work as planned.

In practice, this means every software artifact has to be completely traceable—i.e., which product requirements it addresses, how its specification ensures fulfillment of these requirements and which tests (and test results) prove that its functionality genuinely fulfills its purpose. Later changes to the design or implementation of the product must not reduce or in any other way affect the planned level of safety. This implies that impact analysis has to be performed before changes are made and sugges-

---

8.   That is, the reduction or exclusion of risk to the user and the environment.

tions have to be made regarding how a potential reduction in safety can be counteracted. Every stage of every change also has to be traceable from its proposal through the results of impact analysis to the results of applying it to the product.

Because agile projects involve constant change, it is not easy to guarantee traceability within an agile development process. If the traceability mechanism is complex or unreliable, it will quickly end up producing either a lot of paperwork or traceability gaps. The team also has to consider the level of granularity on which traceability is to be guaranteed. The minimum requirement is to be able to follow the connections between product requirements and system test cases, thus making it possible to use passed tests to prove that the requirements have been fulfilled[9]. For this process to be successful, you have to be able to justify why one or more system test cases are capable of validating the fulfillment of a requirement. This means that the appropriateness of the system test cases has to be checked. If defects are revealed, a reliable analysis and correction process (usually governed by a defect management system) has to take place. In order to trace a defect back to its source, a defect message has to be linked with the test that produced it. In practice, reliable traceability can only be guaranteed if you use appropriately linked requirement and test management tools.

Traceability

At a first glance, it may appear beneficial that this level of formalism is only required for an external release. However, because an agile team often only decides at the end of a Sprint whether the resulting product is to be used extrenally, it doesn't really help. Documenting traceability data after the event is not to be recommended, and it is essential to ensure that builds produced without the use of a working traceability mechanism don't end up being unintentionally delivered. It is always preferable for the traceability mechanism to be a standard part of every Sprint.

Whether traceability on a requirements/system testing level is sufficient and whether more granular artifacts should be included depends on the level at which design decisions are made[10] and the level of the software architecture on which the corresponding functionality is observable (and on which test cases reside). This means that, in some cases, the development process has to be traceable all the way down to the unit testing level.

---

9.   This process is equivalent to the validation step in the V-model.
10. Some compliance requirements determine this level in advance.

7.3.3   Product Attribute Requirements

Software-related compliance issues don't only affect software development activities. The use of software as part of an organization's IT infrastructure, too, can be affected by compliance requirements such as data protection and archiving (including data storage and recovery). Industries that manufacture software-based, safety-related products often have to have the tools they use for the engineering process certified before they are used for the first time and after every update.

This means that software manufacturers have to be familiar with the compliance requirements that prevail in their customers' industries and support them using either dedicated product features or by providing appropriate support services. Features that are designed to fulfill standards don't have to be treated any differently from regular features but will probably be given a higher priority anyway. Close cooperation with the customer and the regular production of working builds makes it easier for agile teams than it is for teams who employ traditional development methodology to identify and fine-tune additional support services and to provide these to the customer in a timely fashion.

The regulations that some industries are subject to (for example, FDA OTS and FDA Validation for medical technology) dictate not only that third-party system software but also specific tools have to be formally validated. The customer effort involved in such validation can significantly slow down an agile development team's work, as every release (and sometimes every patch) has to be validated. Longer release cycles reduce the effort involved, so if the agile team delivers too often, the customer is likely to ignore or skip some versions. In both cases, the team receives no useful feedback from the customer, who may also feel subjected to unwanted pressure to update. In such cases, development based on the traditional V-model is perhaps preferable.

7.4   Traditional Quality Assurance

While quality management (QM) is concerned with the content, quality and optimization of business processes, quality assurance (QA) concentrates on the quality of the products the organization manufactures.

7.4.1 QA Tools

Traditional software development methods differentiate between constructive and analytical QA measures. A template that ensures that a document is constructed in a particular way is an example of constructive QA, as is a pattern used to design software according to an established best practice. All types of testing, checking, reviewing and analysis are classed as analytical QA measures.

Traditionally managed projects describe, plan and apply QA measures *QA and test planning* that are often based on the tenets of the [IEEE 730] standard. Such a plan is usually drafted by the project's QA manager, the test manager or the project manager. A QA plan is accompanied by a testing plan (often drafted according to [IEEE 829]). An estimation of the effort involved in applying the QA measures thus planned is then added to the overall project plan.

7.4.2 Organization

Either the test manger or the QA manager is given the job of applying the planned measures. In large projects, this person is assigned a group of colleagues/testers who are then grouped in a sub-project.

This approach produces a clear distinction between development and *Differentiating between* testing staff and, in traditionally managed projects where this distinction *development and testing* is not made, insufficient quality assurance results. This is because project *staff* management and team members concentrate on contributing to the completion of the product, and testing and review tasks supposedly slow the process down. However, a separate QA group will focus exclusively on QA tasks and will be measured only according to how well it performs them and how many defects it helps to discover prior to delivery. This is an advantage of traditional project organization and management that shouldn't be underestimated.

In the course of some projects, the delegation of QA tasks to a dedicated team causes a tangible reduction in attention to and the feeling of responsibility for quality in general. This manifests itself in the omission of unit tests or sloppy testing practices, secure in the knowledge that QA will sort it out. However, such behavior can also be the result of inadequate definition of which part of the team is actually responsible for unit testing. In the end, everyone assumes that everyone else will deal with the issue.

In order to prevent this kind of misunderstanding, the project manager has to make sure that all parts of the team communicate regularly with one another. This can take the form of a Daily Scrum or a Scrum of Scrums with representatives from all the sub-teams involved.

7.5   Agile Quality Assurance

Agile teams are cross-functional (see section 2.1). The entire team is responsible for the product and its quality and there is no formal separation of roles or dedicated QA group that is solely responsible for QA and testing tasks. Each team member contributes his or her own special skills (software architect, programmer, tester, etc.), but is not exclusively tied to that particular role. Everyone is allowed to perform any of the various types of tasks contained in the task board, including QA and testing.

The organizational anchor for QA tasks is lost during the transition to agile practices and—as shown in the following section—needs to be replaced by a methodical anchor if the team is to continue to uphold the quality of the products it builds.

7.5.1   Principles and Tools

Quality assurance in an agile team is based on the principle of "Inspection and Adaptation"[11], and is defined by the Scrum Guide [URL: Scrum Guide] as follows:

- **Inspection**
  Scrum users must frequently inspect Scrum artifacts and progress toward a Sprint Goal to detect undesirable variances. Their inspection should not be so frequent that inspection gets in the way of the work. Inspections are most beneficial when diligently performed by skilled inspectors at the point of work.

- **Adaptation**
  If an inspector determines that one or more aspects of a process deviate outside acceptable limits, and that the resulting product will be unacceptable, the process or the material being processed must be adjusted. An adjustment must be made as soon as possible to minimize further deviation.

---

11. This idea has been added to the Agile Manifesto [URL: Agile Manifesto] as a twelfth guiding principle.

This means that every single artifact has to be inspected! However, unlike in a traditionally managed project, the questions of when and how checks are performed (and by whom) are not planned in advance, and are instead decided afresh for each new Sprint in the course of the Sprint's built-in routine meetings:

- **Sprint Planning meeting** (see section 3.5)
  The tasks required to complete each item in the Sprint Backlog are discussed and defined in the course of the Sprint Planning meeting. The corresponding acceptance criteria will already have been drafted by the Product Owner and included in the Product Backlog (see section 3.3). These take the place of the quality goals and attributes that are separately defined in conventional QA plans. You then have to decide what types of checks are appropriate and necessary to adequately check whether each acceptance criterion has been properly fulfilled. The available tools that the team can select from include all types of analytical quality assurance measures and test types (see chapters 4, 5 and 6) as well as the exploratory tests detailed in section 6.3. If you decide to make comprehensive checks, these need to be drafted in a separate task (e.g., specify and automate test case) that is included in the Sprint Planning and corresponds to the appropriate development task. If a quick read-through, an existing pair programming review or an existing automated regression test is deemed sufficient, the checks can be noted as implicit in the development task itself. QA tasks are thus handled and prioritized exactly the same way as all other tasks and become part of the daily workflow without the need for a separate QA plan.

- **Daily Scrum**
  This daily meeting is used[12] by the team to reflect on the status of the Sprint and update the task board. You have to be able to prove that the agreed done criteria have been fulfilled for every task that is marked as done. If an explicit testing task was defined, this has to be performed and the results (e.g., the test logs) need to be available for inspection. If this isn't possible, the quality goal for the artifact in question has not been achieved and the task cannot be classed as done. If, for example, a feature proves more difficult to implement than originally assumed, this is where any drawbacks will become clear not just to the program-

---

12. "... a 15-minute time-boxed event for the Development Team to synchronize activities and create a plan for the next 24 hours." [URL: Scrum Guide].

mer concerned but also to the whole team. The Daily Scrum therefore serves not only to provide the team with an overview of progress in general, but also to notify them of any issues that individual team members are currently facing. The team members can thus react quickly and help each other. Any current impediments are also discussed during the Daily Scrum, giving the Scrum Master the opportunity to react and implement appropriate solutions. The Daily Scrum therefore addresses product quality and process-related issues.

Sprint Review

A Sprint Review takes place at the end of every Sprint and is used by the team to present and explain the latest product status to the Product Owner and the customer. At this point, the team receives immediate customer feedback on the new product increment. This forum helps the team and the customer to ensure that the product solves the customer's problem. The Sprint Review thus takes the form of an informal validation and provides customer and quality feedback that extends the feedback provided by the usual tests. This information can then be used to implement any necessary corrections to the product and to add any newly discovered process improvements to the Product Backlog.

Sprint Retrospective

The team uses the Sprint Retrospective to discuss process-related issues and ways to improve the development process (see section 7.2.3). This is where process improvement measures that were identified in the Sprint Review or other steps that serve to improve general effectiveness (for example, improving test coverage by using more automated tests) are discussed and prioritized. Implementing such measures serves to stabilize and improve product quality in all the Sprints that follow.

QA through routine and transparency

Even though there is no explicit person or group who is responsible for QA tasks, there are two major reasons why the team doesn't lose sight of QA in the course of the daily workflow. The daily meetings listed above ensure that QA issues are discussed on a daily basis and the basic principles of Scrum ensure that any quality deficits are identified at an early stage. These can be failed tests that show up in the dashboard, task cards that cannot be moved because their done criteria haven't been fulfilled, or comments made by the customer during the Sprint Review. Because the whole team is constantly in touch with the entire development process, many faults are avoided from the start, and the tendency for individual team members to work in isolation is largely eliminated. In a cross-functional team, the twin disciplines of routine meetings and transparency directly replace the individual responsibilities that are assigned to the members of a conventional development team.

7.5.2   Strengths and Weaknesses

A team that puts the agile QA measures described above into practice will usually achieve great results. The strengths of this approach are:

▪ **Every development artifact is tested**
This includes testing executable program code, reviewing and inspecting architecture diagrams, class diagrams and other design documents, and questioning and checking the validity of the project plan via the contents of the task board and Sprint Backlog.

▪ **Corrective measures take place as early as possible**
When an automated test case fails, the cause is analyzed immediately. If possible, the responsible programmer corrects the defect immediately or offers a solution within the current Sprint. If the problem persists, corrective measures (such as a change in product design) are added to the Product Backlog and a suitable solution is set in motion according to the usual prioritization process.

▪ **Constructive QA tools come to the fore**
Techniques such as Clean Code, test automation, Test First etc. clearly raise the level of craftsmanship and technical expertise within the development process. The team develops its own high-quality standards for the product and the techniques it uses to build it.

▪ **Process improvements are made from the bottom up**
Steps are introduced quickly according to the real and immediate needs of the team.

If the team takes advantage of these strengths, it can develop its own disciplined and highly effective QA culture. However, success is not automatic and the Scrum approach also harbors risks when it comes to continually ensuring product quality. It is up to you to decide whether the following points are risks that can be mitigated or whether they represent general weaknesses of the Scrum or agile approach to software development. Whatever you decide, you should definitely know they exist:

Risks of agile QA culture

An ideal world vs. day-to-day reality

Scrum, XP and other agile processes are all based on the concept of cross-functional teams[13]. A Scrum Team is made up of members who between them have all the skills required to reach the Sprint Goal [Schwaber/Beedle 02, page 37]. However, the day-to-day reality of working within an organization is a different ballgame. Required expertise is not always present in the team and some team members are more productive than others, taking on the role of "team player," "maverick," or "guru." If you are thinking of introducing Scrum or you already work in a Scrum Team, you must recognize that your team is not perfect, and assume that it is can easily hinder the potentially smooth processes that Scrum methodology is designed to generate.

Learning vs. Skills

Working in pairs and assisting each other helps all members of the team to improve their skills. This way, the team can add missing skills to its repertoire and give every member the opportunity to share their knowledge while learning new skills of their own. However, in reality, not every team member will be able to work smoothly and effectively with all the others, and not everyone likes to share their expertise. Because Scrum is forced to use "timeboxing" to counteract the time constraints that it implicitly suffers from, time taken to learn new skills is a scarce resource and the team will usually rely on someone who has the appropriate skills rather someone who is still learning when a task has to be finished. Every team member has his or her own specific academic background and starts learning from a different standpoint. It is therefore unlikely (and, from the company's point of view, uneconomical) for team members to learn completely new skills on the job. Where such an approach makes sense, some will manage it, some won't and others simply won't want to try. Generally speaking, utilizing existing strengths is always preferable to trying to eliminate weaknesses[14].

Pull vs. Push

Scrum, XP and other agile models are based on the assumption that the team organizes itself. However, just as there are good or less good project managers and team leaders to be found in the world of tradi-

---

13. In XP [Beck/Andres 04] the concept is called the One Team Principle, whereas Scrum [Schwaber/Beedle 02] refers to a cross-functional team.
14. Fredmund Malik sees using known strengths as the most important of his six principles of effective leadership (see [Malik 09, chapter 4]).

tionally managed projects, some agile teams are better at organizing themselves than others. The factors that can hinder effective self-organization are manifold. As in other environments, Scrum projects, too, are made up of a variety of tasks that range from interesting and exciting to positively humdrum, and this is a factor that is sure to influence Sprint Planning and Backlog refinement. Of course, the team will ensure that unpopular tasks are not completely ignored but still won't automatically prevent more interesting tasks from gaining a higher priority than necessary, just as some team members will (consciously or subconsciously) pick the more interesting tasks from those currently being offered. In spite of the "pull" principle on which Scrum is based, a "push" or two on the part of the Product Owner or a particular team member is still sometimes prudent! Like any other team, a Scrum Team will also incorporate some ambitious and capable members, and some are more likely than others to raise their hands and push things along. Such undercurrents can lead to the formation of unofficial hierarchies within the team that are actually quite similar to those of a traditional project team. The team may be able to live with this, but might at some point find that it is no longer a Scrum Team at all.

Discipline vs. Velocity

Working to the rhythm of organized Sprints might appear to be a simple, pleasant and well-regulated affair. However, the strict adherence to the rules of transparency and the permanent timeboxing involved in reaching the immovable goal of the end of the Sprint can generate quite a lot of pressure. Theoretically, the team uses Sprint Planning to regulate the amount of work so that a constant Team Velocity that the team can keep up is established. In practice, however, you will often find that discipline is instead sacrificed for the sake of speed. The principles of Test First are not consistently applied due to a lack of time to practice; no one writes traditional longhand specifications, if only because documentation is a fundamentally non-agile process; test cases that could be automated are applied manually because there is no time to automate them; necessary (or desirable) refactoring is delayed because the customer's top priority is new features, etc. This all pushes the team into a downward spiral that leads eventually to a failed project.

Every Scrum Master and agile team will have to face these or similar risks that don't only affect the effectiveness of the QA process. However, the strengths of agile QA processes listed at the beginning of this section can only be brought to bear if these risks are kept under control.

7.6 Agile Testing

Even if constructive measures take on a high priority within an agile team, testing is still the most important quality assurance tool there is. Chapters 4, 5 and 6 describe in detail what testing is capable of and how testing is approached in an agile development environment. The following sections summarize the critical factors that make testing agile.

7.6.1 Critical Factors for Successful Agile Testing

Agile testing is the testing of software within an agile development project [...] Agile testing follows the principles laid out in the Agile Manifesto and applies the principles of agile methodology to software testing (after [URL: Agile Testing]).

Nonstop testing with daily feedback   The main demand made of an agile tester is that he/she provides timely feedback, and all testing efforts are made with this goal in mind. Instead of sequential testing phases (and correspondingly slow feedback), continuous, parallel testing takes place during every Sprint, providing nonstop testing with daily feedback. The following factors are critical to the success of this approach:

▪ **Test automation**
  Timely feedback can only be provided continually if all tests (i.e., unit, integration and system tests) are sufficiently automated. Such a network of automated tests enables continuous refactoring of the program code and is a necessary prerequisite for the reliable application of this Clean Code approach (see [Martin 08]).

▪ **Exploratory testing**
  Because it is not possible to automate every test case immediately, additional (quick) manual testing is required. This is achieved using exploratory testing—a technique that does largely without a preparatory test specification and gives the tester the freedom to work intuitively, thus enabling extremely short-term testing of new features whose expected behavior is still only roughly outlined on the appropriate task card. This also means that the tester has to be capable of actively approach-

ing all stakeholders and other potential sources of test data. This technique requires talent, but can be learned.

Test expertise within the team

The responsibility for testing lies within an agile team. Test activities are planned and controlled the same way as all other activities within a Sprint. Each member of the team can (and should) carry out testing tasks according to his/her own individual skills. Making testing a team task requires the team to have appropriate skills from the start, and a traditional development team that switches to using Scrum methodology is not usually appropriately skilled. In most cases, external testers or members of an existing system testing team will be seconded to the Scrum Team to bolster its testing capabilities. These people then have to learn to test as part of an agile team rather than in the independent testing environment they are accustomed to. Independent testing with separately defined roles and separate organizational structures is abandonded. This switch is not without risk and can only succeed if you make sure that the team also includes its own testing experts and that the Scrum Master or a test specialist adopts the role of test manager. However, even if the team includes testing experts, the close cooperation inherent in an agile team can weaken the testing process because (as recounted in case study 8.1) even full-time testers tend to see the project increasingly from a developer's point of view and, as a result, assess test results less critically than an independent tester might.

Multiple teams

If multiple Scrum Teams are working on a single project (as Feature Teams), you need to take a more general view to ensure that all features under development continue to work together properly. Even if the individual teams perform unit, integration and system tests for their features, you run the risk of neglecting comprehensive system-wide testing. To counteract this tendency, the test manager and full-time testers need to meet regularly and exchange views the way Scrum Masters do in the Scrum of Scrums. This exchange could take the form of a Scrum of Testers, as described in case study 8.3. It might also make sense to form an overarching system testing team (see section 6.8.1) that not only ensures that inter-team test scenarios exist but also maintains the test frameworks and provides them to other teams as a service.

7.6.2   Test Planning in Scrum

As already mentioned, testing activities in a Scrum project are planned and controlled the same way as all other activities within a Sprint—using tasks that are shifted from the Product Backlog to the Sprint Backlog and then to the task board in the course of Sprint Planning. The following points need to be considered when planning Scrum-based tests:

▪ **Definition of Ready (DoR)**
The team's DoR is a checklist that the Product Owner uses to write and assure the quality of the User Stories and that is referred to when Stories are pulled from the Product Backlog to the Sprint Backlog. The team can tell if a User Story is Ready by viewing it from a tester's point of view. If you cannot draft adequate test cases or if it is not clear when to class a test result as passed or failed, the Story is obviously not sufficiently well defined and should be rejected as not Ready. Alternatively, the team can fill the gaps in the Story by applying the principles of Test First and adding test cases that deliver the missing results. Having the Product Owner work in a pair with a tester is a great way to get this particular job done.

▪ **Definition of Done (DoD)**
The DoD is an additional checklist that describes the goals the team has to reach before a Story can be classified as ready for inclusion in the Sprint Review. The DoD includes factors such as the required test types and test coverage, and the criteria that define a test as done (usually the elimination of all defects). The DoD is therefore directly involved in assuring product quality and customer satisfaction.

A testing task can be explicitly defined as a separate task, or it can exist implicitly in the form of a done criterion for a programming task. If all the necessary tests have already been written and automated, taking the implicit approach presents no problems—however, when a Story or feature is being tested for the first time (or tests are in the process of being automated), it is advisable to handle such tasks separately and explicitly.

7.7   **Skills, Training, Values**

In the course of the past 10 years, software testing has become a profession in its own right. Many projects entrust their testing and QA activities to Certified Testers who then play a significant role in the success of the project.

High levels of software testing and QA skills are essential in the increasingly complex systems being built by today's (agile) software development teams. Agile testing doesn't mean testing less or less stringently than before and, in fact, takes on a highly significant role. Test cases define the system in the place of specifications (Test First), tests are automated as far as possible and performed continuously (Nonstop testing). Designing high-quality test cases is a demanding task that requires special training. Test automation requires programming and test tool know-how, as do code analysis, Continuous Integration, reviewing techniques, etc.

High levels of QA and software testing skills are essential.

Because Scrum doesn't explicitly define the tester role and doesn't even mention the role of test manager, Scrum Teams often lack the skills required to successfully perform software tests. This is a risky situation, since Scrum relies heavily on feedback loops and tests are one of the most important sources of feedback in a software development environment.

All members of a cross-functional team are affected, so it is essential that everyone involved—including the programmers—has at least basic testing skills. Conversely, to enable them to perform test automation and code analysis tasks, testers also have to be conversant with the basics of programming. All these techniques require practice and the personnel department has to agree with the Scrum Master and the QM staff (see section 7.2.2) on a training schedule for the team.

The internationally accepted qualification for software testers is the ISTQB Certified Tester standard. The Foundation Level syllabus covers all basic techniques, from equivalence partitioning via boundary value analysis to state-based testing, thus addressing all stages of the process that a Scrum Team is sure to be confronted with, from unit tests to acceptance testing (see chapters 4, 5 and 6). The ISTQB Advanced and Expert Level syllabi go into greater depth and are suitable for team members who are specifically involved in testing and QA. The syllabi are published by the ISTQB and its national testing boards, who are also responsible for testing itself and monitoring the training courses on offer [URL: ISTQB].

ISTQB Certified Testers

If you are already a Certified Tester, you should consider taking a course in the basics of Scrum, perhaps combined with agile testing tech-

Training agile testing techniques

niques (for example, "Testing in SCRUM" [URL: iAkad] or the Certified Agile Tester course [URL: iCAT]). The reference syllabus for such courses is the new ISTQB "Foundation Level Extension Syllabus Agile Tester" [URL: ISTQB]. Courses that concentrate on individual testing techniques such as exploratory testing are a useful addition (but not an alternative) to ISTQB Foundation Level training. As we have already shown, testing within an agile project requires know-how that covers the entire spectrum of testing techniques—exploratory techniques are just one part of the puzzle.

Change your values　　Switching to Scrum involves changing the way you work. From the point of view of quality management and assurance processes, there are two changes that are particularly evident. Quality management especially is transformed from a top-down into a bottom-up process and the QM team provides a service to the agile team. Operative quality assurance (QA) is no longer a task performed by an external team and instead becomes an integral part of the Scrum Team's workflow. These changes necessarily involve a change in the values of the testers and QA specialists who work in an agile team:

- Constructive relations between team members are more important than test processes and tools.
- Tested software is more important than comprehensive test documentation.
- Continuous collaboration with the customer is more important than formal acceptance tests performed at the end of the project.
- Reacting to change is more important than following a rigid test plan.

The necessary soft skills that can usefully accompany these attitudes are cooperation, pairing, communication rather than documentation, self-organization, initiative and active information search and retrieval.

This makes the methodical skills of experienced testing and QA specialists more important than ever. The way you work is sure to change, and at imbus, we say:

"Change your MindSet! Keep Your MethodSet!

7.8   Questions and Exercises

7.8.1   Self-Assessment

Questions and exercises to help you assess how agile your project or team really is.

1. How well does your company's QM system work? Do real-world practice and QM rules coincide, or do they form two parallel universes?
2. Are the rules current? When was the system last updated?
3. Are your own tasks and responsibilities adequately defined? Do you follow the rules for your personal responsibilities?
4. Are you familiar with all the QM documents that are relevant to your responsibilities? How long does it take you to find and refer to a particular document?
5. How are new or altered processes implemented? Are there appropriate information or training sessions?
6. How is the software development process defined? Which phase of the process are you currently involved in? Which criteria have to apply in order to end the current phase?
7. If you have taken part in an audit, what were the outcomes and have you since introduced any corrective measures?
8. How effective is cooperation between your department/team and the QM staff? Where would agile practices help?
9. If your team(s) already use agile practices, how good is cooperation between the Scrum Master and the QM staff? Are the topics addressed in the Sprint Retrospectives effectively implemented? How could implementation be improved?
10. Which analytical QA measures (apart from testing) and which constructive measures do you use in your project? Which measures or techniques are not used although they make sense? Why?
11. If your team(s) already use agile practices, how is testing organized? How well do the team(s) fulfill the Critical Factors for Successful Agile Testing?
12. How does your project's testing plan look at the moment? Can you use it to identify which testing tasks are pending today/this week? Are these the tasks that actually get done? Do they help to find the right defects on time?

7.8.2   Methods and Techniques

These questions will help you to review the content of the current chapter.

1. Explain the term "PDCA cycle."
2. With reference to the project plan shown in fig. 2-3, which PDCA cycles can you identify?
3. With reference to the Scrum process shown in fig. 2-1, which PDCA cycles can you identify?
4. Explain the difference between a Team Charter and a QM-based description of the agile development process.
5. Explain the Sprint Review and Sprint Retrospective Scrum tools.
6. What does traceability mean? Why do the relevant standards for software development in safety-related products require a high degree of traceability?
7. List the advantages and disadvantages of separating developers and testers and the tasks they perform.
8. Explain the agile principle "inspect and adapt."
9. List the advantages and disadvantages of cross-functional teams. What are the risks involved?
10. Name and explain the factors that are critical to successful agile testing.

7.8.3   Other Exercises

These exercises will help you delve deeper into topics touched on in the course of the chapter.

1. Regardless of whether you work traditionally or using agile methodology, describe the software development process you use in a maximum of one page.
2. Select a second software project or team that you are familiar with and describe the differences between the methods it uses and the ones you described in the previous exercise. Generalize your process description so that it covers both sets of characteristics.
3. If you are working on an agile project, describe in the style of a Team Charter (see section 3.6) how Sprint Planning and effort estimation in your team work. Does this description apply to other teams too, or just yours?

8 Case Studies

This chapter presents case studies featuring industrial, e-commerce and software companies. Each study reviews the experiences made and lessons learned by the interviewees in the course of introducing and implementing agile practices in their respective organizations.

8.1 Using Scrum to Develop Video and Audio Production Software

An interview with Dr. Stephan Albrecht,
Manager of Interplay Escalation and Tools at AVID in Munich, Germany

AVID was founded in 1987 near Boston in the USA. It is a NASDAQ-listed company that develops and sells digital audio and video production solutions. The company's range of products ranges from digital video-editing systems for end-users (Pinnacle Studio, Avid Studio) to professional movie and TV production systems such as Avid Interplay and Avid Media Composer. Many of the most successful advertisements, music videos, TV shows, and movies in the world are produced using AVID products.

Working in such a dynamic environment, the company has to develop complex, high-end software within short innovation cycles, and any defects in the product are quite literally audible and visible to the customer.

Because of the nature of its products, AVID has always used strongly iterative development methods and, in 2009, decided to take the plunge and introduce Scrum. This case study describes the company's experiences introducing Scrum into the Media and Production Asset Management business unit, which employs approximately 100 developers working in Burlington, Kiev, Shanghai, Kaiserslautern, and Munich.

Reasons for Switching to Scrum

The traditional iterative approach saw development taking place in various independent teams working in a variety of locations. For example, the Munich office had a design team, multiple development teams and its own system testing and quality management team. A product manager was responsible for project planning and decided which features were to be included in each release.

Generally, the iterative approach worked well, but it was still felt that the various teams didn't talk to each other enough, resulting in misunderstandings and avoidable defects. It was also obvious that, regardless of how often and how comprehensively they were drawn up and revised, the project plans never really caught up with the reality of the everyday production workflow. Introducing Scrum was the obvious way to address both issues and had the potential to accelerate and improve the quality of work in general.

Transition

The original design, development and quality management teams were dissolved and reformed as cross-functional teams with new responsibilities. Now, each team has all the necessary skills and is responsible for developing a particular product. In other words, each team has its own designers, developers, testers and quality management specialists. The team leaders were trained externally as Scrum Masters and each took over a team as Scrum Master and line manager.

Obstacles

The Scrum Masters initially fell back into their old team leader habits and were too dominant in their new roles. This became particularly obvious when planned features weren't ready at the end of a Sprint. Team members were unhappy with the way the Scrum Master had attempted to force completion of the affected features even though it was clear from the start that this wasn't possible. In such cases, the Scrum Masters simply decided that certain features were to be completed within the Sprint by a specific person, the same way they did as team leaders.

Filling the role of Product Owner also generated some difficulties. The highly complex nature of the products and the enormous number of features they contain meant that only a very few people could be considered for the job—once again, the first choice was usually the former team leader. This meant that some of the new Scrum Masters also took on (or were given) the role of Product Owner or Proxy Product Owner (i.e., the Product Owner's local contact).

Both of these issues were remedied. Management selected a single Product Owner who was responsible for Product Backlog refinement for the entire Media and Production Asset Management unit. The same person was also made responsible for determining the timing and content of external releases, and thus Sprint Planning too. The Scrum Masters gradually adapted their leadership skills to the new situation, and those who weren't up to the change were replaced by other team members. Various working methods and resources that served to improve communication between teams (for example, the form of the Backlogs and the burndown charts) were standardized across all teams.

Major Changes

The old matrix-style organization (departments × projects) was replaced by multi-functional teams so that skills (such as system testing) that used to be provided centrally ended up being the responsibility of the individual teams. Each team synchronizes its work by way of a daily standup meeting, and team synchronization is handled using a Scrum of Scrums video conference.

As expected, the teams were initially missing some of the skills (such as quality management) that used to be provided by specialized departments. This made work in the new Scrum Teams more varied but also more demanding for the affected team members. Gaps in team members' experience can be bridged by other team members who are asked to help out for a day or two, but every team member has to acquire appropriate skills sooner or later.

With the exception of a few special branches, code no longer belongs to the individual developers but instead to the entire team. This means that everyone is allowed to adapt and develop all the program code. Some team members see this as a loss of responsibility while others see it as an opportunity to get to grips with new aspects of a familiar product. Nevertheless, because the complexity of the products makes them prone to defects, AVID doesn't allow inter-team code ownership, so colleagues from outside of a team are not allowed to edit code. The coordination between teams that this would entail would be too complex anyway. In some cases, the code and its associated skills are so highly specialized that code ownership for certain parts of the product remains with designated specialists.

There were changes to requirements engineering too. A User Story Ready status was introduced, which means that a User Story (or its dependent feature tasks) can only be added to the Sprint Backlog if the User Story Ready status is fulfilled. This ensures that half-baked User Stories don't end up impeding the Sprint.

Changes to the Testing Procedures

Testers used to be members of a system testing team within a central quality assurance department. This department was dissolved and system test automation specialists, automated unit test specialists, manual system testers and performance testers now work on their own within the individual Scrum Teams. In the short term, this means that testing staff still require access to the specialist skills of the former quality assurance staff. However, this situation also gives team members the opportunity to learn new skills and share their testing know-how. Some team members who used to work as testers (usually unit testers) now write code too, while other former system testers have expanded their skills to include providing user support and writing user documentation. It has proved comparatively difficult to get former developers to adapt to performing testing tasks. The focus of many AVID developers still lies within an individual feature and the details of its implementation.

Lessons Learned

- The introduction of Scrum has shortened internal release cycles (i.e., Sprints) from between one and three months to one month or less. However, not every Sprint results in an external release.
- All work is strongly focused on tasks committed to by the team.
- In turn, this means that tasks are sometimes chosen arbitrarily from the Backlog, which leads to short-term progress in individual customer-oriented features taking priority over essential long-term base functionality and stabilization work.
- The dissolution of the old team structure is a real boon. Developers and testers now work hand in hand and continually provide each other with feedback. This results in faster reactions to internal and external defect reports.

- On the downside, bug tracking is now only possible for issues that affect multiple teams or Sprints. All other bugs are not documented but are instead handled quickly and informally within teams, making it more difficult than it used to be to identify problem hotspots.

- The close cooperation with the developers and the increasing slant of the testers' work toward programming sometimes creates a developer mindset among testers. Some testers begin to see things from a developer's point of view, and make statements that begin, "We can't do that because …." We have also noticed that some testers don't like to stand up in the Daily Scrum at the end of a Sprint and tell the team that a feature isn't done.

- The increased transparency provided by the Backlog and the task cards on the whiteboard helps everyone. Avid's open company culture has helped team members who used to be quite reserved to contribute happily to morning standup meetings.

- Development of base functionality has to take place incrementally too and, ideally, delivers new, customer-centric functionality at the end of every Sprint.

- The degree of test automation has increased enormously. However, multiple tests are difficult to automate economically, so we now perform an additional Test Sprint before each external release. This consists of complex, mostly manual tests that cannot be performed for every build.

- Errors and misunderstandings haven't been completely cleared up but are identified and remedied faster on all levels.

- If something doesn't work, we react immediately and correct the process concerned, even if this means deviating from a Scrum-by-the-book approach. For example, at the time this interview was conducted, we were involved in checking the independence of our tests and how to improve test uniformity. These considerations involve performing release Sprints in teams that are put together temporarily for this purpose. Also, because centralized standards still work better in some contexts, we are considering whether to re-introduce centralized system testing and quality assurance responsibilities. We are still discussing how best to approach this change.

Conclusions

Overall, Stephan Albrecht draws positive conclusions, and tells us, "The close cooperation between developers and testers and the short development iterations this enables are major advantages of using Scrum. However, this approach also demands that testers remain extremely objective with regard to the objects they are testing."

8.2 Nonstop System Testing— Using Scrum to Develop the Test*Bench* Tool

*An interview with Joachim Hofer, Test*Bench *Development Manager and Dierk Engelhardt, Test*Bench *Product Manager at imbus AG*

imbus AG is a German company specializing in software quality assurance and testing. At the time of writing, imbus had more than 200 employees working at locations in Germany, Sousse/Tunisia, and Shanghai, China. The company offers consulting, software testing and test outsourcing services as well as its own testing tools and training. Its customers are software manufacturers and the software development departments of government agencies and companies in all branches of industry.

Test*Bench* is a powerful test management tool developed by imbus. It covers all aspects of the testing process, from planning, design and automation to test execution and reporting of all software testing tasks. Test*Bench* is used by customers in medical technology, railway engineering, the automobile industry and in banking and insurance.

The tool was developed using Java by a team comprising between 12 and 16 members. The product is implemented and integrated at customer sites by specialist Test*Bench* consultants. Until 2010, the product was developed using an iterative, phase-oriented process with programmers and testers working in separate groups and producing one or two major releases per year.

Improvement Goals

This development process caused the typical issues that phase-oriented models are known for. System testing only began once implementation was complete and programmers were already celebrating the completed iteration. The system testers regularly dampened the programmers' enthusiasm with a series of defect reports. From the programmers' point of view, these reports came unnecessarily late and often addressed issues that required intervention for which there was no additional time available in the current iteration. Each iteration was therefore separated into an implementation phase and a subsequent bug-fixing phase, with the latter taking place under enormous pressure because of the limited time available and the need to succeed. The result was a high-quality, stable product but the development process was always an uphill struggle.

To alleviate this situation, the goal of parallelizing programming and testing was set. The idea was to provide more timely testing feedback to the programmers and further automate the testing process to provide greater code refactoring safety for the future of the product's development.

Introducing Agile Development Techniques

Starting in 2010, development manager Joachim Hofer began introducing a whole raft of agile practices in order to reach these goals:

- **Requirements management**
  Previously, a requirement took the form of a headline in the *Caliber* requirement management tool that was linked to a detailed *Word* document. Implementation could only begin once the entire document had been approved. The decision was made to move away from large requirements documents and instead to rely on smaller User Stories built up successively and logged using the *Jira* issue management tool.

- **Nightly build**
  The rules for the production of nightly builds were also tightened. A central compilation and integration environment already existed and the programmers logged in their code whenever it was ready (on average, every two or three days). This approach created a certain amount of unfinished code that was not yet checked in, so the decision was made to have all programmers check in all their code every evening. The existing automated unit tests were then performed on the complete code, which initially led to all sorts of problems. However, the result was an important learning experience that taught the team to work daily toward finished, executable code. The packets of code that the programmers tackled each morning became smaller and the planned changes were mostly complete by evening.

Nightly automated system tests

In addition to further automating unit testing, the team pushed ahead with the automation of system testing too. The test environment was extended so that the unit and integration tests were followed by nightly automated system tests started directly from the build environment. All new system tests were designed immediately and implemented using the *QF-Test* tool so that they could be included in the nightly test environment.

Continuous Integration

Originally, each build took four hours to produce, which was just doable in the context of a nightly build but still too slow to ensure that the nightly tests were complete before work began the next day. The build time was reduced to 15 minutes by separating each build into a series of sub-projects and rebuilding the build environment as a Jenkins/Hudson environment. All automated unit, integration and (nightly build) system tests were repackaged and embedded in the improved build environment. Depending on the test package being run, feedback times were reduced to a minimum of 15 minutes—i.e., no longer than a coffee break!

Static code analysis and coverage measurement

The dynamic unit tests in the continuous integration (CI) environment were extended to include additional static code analysis that runs parallel to automated integration testing. For example, the *FindBugs* tool is used to identify typical Java coding issues such as incorrect API calls.

Task orientation

To achieve sufficiently granular task control within each iteration, task-oriented working methods based on User Stories were introduced. To prioritize tasks, a scoring system was introduced that evaluates task priority using the customer's viewpoint, the number of corresponding customer requirements and an internal vote within the team.

Daily Standup

The team now meets for 15 minutes every morning. Each team member reports on what he/she is doing right now, how work is progressing and on any current issues. Everyone decides for themselves which tasks to report. As yet, there is no real Sprint Planning to compare with the reported tasks, but the daily nature of the meeting makes great practice for a forthcoming Daily Scrum.

All these practices were introduced while preserving the original iterative development model. However, the use of User Stories and continuous integration (CI) went a long way toward dissolving the strict phases of the earlier development process and helped to interlace and parallelize them. The next step involved introducing agile product and project management practices and transforming the team into a self-organized unit.

Introducing Scrum

The new development techniques listed above were introduced largely by development manager Joachim Hofer. The time had now come to involve the whole team in the Scrum process. Joachim Hofer and product manager Dierk Engelhardt decided to make the switch in the course of several individual steps:

- **Research and inform**
  Kanban, Scrum, XP and other agile methodologies were considered, but the discussion and the planning that followed quickly focused on Scrum. An internal forum was set up in which the team could add its thoughts and make suggestions regarding how to set up the new Scrum-based development process. Spurred on by their own curiosity, all team members studied current Scrum literature and visited websites such as scrum.org to get an idea of what Scrum is all about. This process was accompanied by internal workshops and regular team discussions.

- **Restructuring the team**
  The switch to Scrum of course required a change of roles, responsibilities and tasks within the team. Joachim Hofer became the Scrum Master, the test manager became his deputy, and the product manager took on the role of Product Owner. The division between testers and programmers was abolished and pair programming was introduced with tester/developer pairs usually responsible for testing and integration tasks, pairs of two developers for development tasks and pairs of testers for system testing tasks.

- **Sprints**
  There is no ideal or easy moment to give up your old development habits and start the first Sprint—you simply have to go for it. At imbus, the first Sprint Planning meeting took place on a Monday early in 2011. The Product Owner had already transferred what he considered to be

the most important requirements from the old project plan to the Project Backlog, which the team turned into a set of task cards for a four-week Sprint during an initial one-day Sprint Planning session. The team later switched to a three-week Sprint cycle.

Major Changes

- The dissolution of the differences between the traditional roles of testers and programmers and the adoption of the role of all-round team members was generally acknowledged as the most serious change. The introduction of pair programming played an important role in making the transition successful.
- Pair programming made code reviews a regular part of the workflow. Every programmer hands over new code to his/her partner for review as a matter of course. This practice also stimulates the sharing of know-how within the team.
- The milestone/work package approach to task planning was replaced by a task-oriented approach to task management. This reduced the importance of the *Caliber* requirement management tool and increased the importance of the *Jira* issue management tool and the *Greenhopper* plug-in (for Backlog management, task ranking, task board management and metrics/charts).
- The main Scrum tools Backlog, Sprint Planning/Planning Poker, time-boxing and Retrospectives were successfully introduced and have been practiced since in a sustained and disciplined fashion.
- User Stories enabled the introduction of stricter development rules. From the very start, the team has had to write test cases for every code change or new User Story in *Jira*. Previously, team members were allowed to write tests once a change in code had been completed. Now, a programmer/tester pair is responsible for writing unit, integration or system tests for each User Story in advance. The programmers then use the *TestNG* tool to implement and execute unit and integration tests, while the testers automate the system tests using *QF-Test*.
- The introduction of CI enables parallelization of programming and testing tasks as planned. Every time a change in code is checked into the system, a build run results. This consists of a minimum of compilation and unit tests and it takes about three minutes for feedback to reach the programmer. Integration tests lasting 15-30 minutes follow.

- In addition to the CI runs that are triggered by the programmers' code check-ins and take place several times a day, the team also makes a nightly build. Each run involves starting a virtual machine with a freshly installed operating system and installing the last successful version of the product to emerge from the CI process. Automated system testing controlled by Test*Bench* follows, and currently comprises about 15,000 data-driven test steps that take approximately 10 hours to complete. The code is automatically instrumented in advance and currently achieves about 40% line coverage. Video captures of the nightly system tests are made that enable staff to follow failed tests visually the next morning. Total code coverage within the CI environment is about 60% and reaches almost 100% for newly implemented features or User Stories. Older code for which no automated tests exist unfortunately reduces overall coverage.

- The test specifications used previously were largely replaced by commented test code and, for the system tests, by keyword-driven, machine-executable test specifications. Test*Bench* is closely linked to *Jira* and the Jenkins environment and is used to successfully manage all system tests.

- The system tests are not completely automated and manual testing will, in future, still be necessary for checking report graphs, usability, etc., so an additional half-day, session-based exploratory system test takes place at the end of each Sprint. The switch from iterative to agile development has nevertheless drastically reduced the manual testing effort from several person-weeks to one person-day every three weeks.

- Sprints are three weeks long and result in a tested internal product release. As previously, external releases take place twice a year. Changes in customer requirements can be handled right up to the start of the last Sprint (i.e., as little as three weeks before delivery).

Lessons Learned

- The introduction of agile development techniques (such as continuous integration) before we switched to using Scrum gave us a stable base on which to build all of our Sprints right from the very start.

- Setting up the tool infrastructure (mainly for CI) involved significant effort that shouldn't be underestimated. Setup work definitely reduces the potential feature productivity of the first few Sprints.

- Pair programming is crucial to the team's success, although some team members find it easier to work with certain colleagues and do not harmonize with everyone. Pairs have to be allowed to form themselves and cannot be forced to work together.
- Test-driven development improves the overall code architecture, and the number of defects that have to be managed has been significantly reduced.
- Regular Sprint Retrospectives deliver a continuous stream of ideas on how to improve things (e.g., improved effort estimation or discussion of questions like "What exactly is a Story Point?").
- Scrum does not reduce the overall workload and does not create additional resources! However, work that is done really is finished. We no longer have to deal with large numbers of defects and painstaking rounds of bug fixing.
- Product roadmaps are replaced by strategic planning.
- Switching to Scrum requires commitment on the part of the team managers and the team, and takes time. It also requires research, training and the setup of new infrastructure that cannot be accomplished overnight.

Conclusions

After a year's experience with Scrum, Dierk Engelhardt and Joachim Hofer confirmed that they were able to reach the goals they set out to achieve. The team now uses important agile techniques, such as test-driven development and continuous integration, in a disciplined and sustained fashion. Their test-driven development and zero defect strategies are particularly effective and the integration of Test*Bench* and Jenkins have made nonstop testing (i.e., continuous automated unit, integration and system testing) a reality. Comprehensive refactoring has also become much less of a risk and the effort involved in producing an external release has been significantly reduced. The team is really happy with the new arrangements.

However, the team isn't content to rest on its laurels and the next improvements to the development process are already being planned. These include the use of *Atlassian Confluence* to describe the system requirements and further acceleration of the CI process through test parallelization and upgrades to the build and test server hardware.

8.3   Using Scrum to Develop an Online Store

An interview with Sabine Herrmann,
Agile Tester at zooplus AG in Munich

zooplus AG is an e-commerce company involved in retail sales of all kinds of products for pets and their owners. The company offers a total of around 8,000 products for dogs, cats, birds, reptiles, horses, small rodents, and fish, including branded foods, own-brand products, toys, care products and a variety of other accessories. The company's website also includes a range of free information on veterinary topics as well as interactive applications, forums and blogs.

The company was founded in 1999 and focused initially on the German and Austrian markets, but has been continually expanding into other European markets since 2005. The company's turnover has grown at an annual rate of 33% for the past four years and the number of employees has grown to match.

zooplus AG currently employs 200 people, 51 of whom work in IT and 102 in marketing.

How Things Were

The rapid growth the company has seen in the last 10 years has seen its IT infrastructure expand rapidly, too.

Before the switch to Scrum in 2008, there were separate store and back-end development teams for the company's nine online stores. There was also a separate team responsible for testing new store functionality (integration testing) and basic functionality (regression testing).

Development at that time followed a traditional three-phase model:
Development → Testing → Production.

Existing issues before the switch:

- There was no clearly defined change management process.
- There was no real coordination between the development and testing teams (for example, to oversee version management issues).
- There were too many highly specialized experts at work and not enough team-based effort.
- In step with the company, the functionality of the software had grown quickly, making regression testing increasingly complex.

Switching to Scrum

The switch to Scrum took place in two phases:

Phase 1

The store and back-end teams began to use Scrum artifacts in the context of Daily Scrum meetings, two Scrum Masters were named and the *Jira* bug-tracking tool was introduced. Requirements were documented in a dedicated Wiki.

Phase 2

New, cross-functional teams were formed with the help of Scrum Coaches and finally, toward the end of 2009, the "big bang" occurred and the team switched completely to Scrum.

The first few Sprints were performed by three Scrum Teams working on the premise that every team can do everything and moving away from isolated expertise. This process was accompanied by many discussions about the new requirement documentation and change management processes.

The following issues became apparent after the switch:

▨ Not all departments were involved in the introduction of the new processes, making the changes in the software development process less transparent than they could have been.
▨ The external testing team wasn't properly involved and was consequently faced with the new challenge of performing tests for all three teams.
▨ One Product Owner wasn't sufficient to cover the work of three teams, so the teams ended up doing a lot of their own analysis during the Sprints.

The positive effects of the switch were:

▨ The dissolution of the insular distribution of expertise.
▨ The use of Sprints and the Product Backlog provided increased transparency in the development process for management and all other stakeholders.
▨ Software features became easier to plan.
▨ Early testing improved quality.
▨ Existing working habits were broken.

- Domain-based knowledge is now available within the individual expert teams.
- A new emphasis on teamwork and Scrum techniques prevailed.
- Synchronization between the teams was significantly improved.

How Things Are Today

Constant requirement growth has led to corresponding growth in the IT department and development now takes place in five Scrum Teams.

There was a lot of discussion and resistance during the switch to Scum, but no one actually ended up leaving the company. Today, change is generally more easily accepted. The teams work differently and the Retrospectives that take place at the end of each project have helped to establish a process of constant change and improvement.

The external testing team was no longer able to cover all testing tasks for five separate Scrum Teams, so the role of agile tester was introduced in each team.

Agile testing led to the complete eradication of the separate development and test phases and the ability to complete the Story within each Sprint. Testing the acceptance criteria is now an integral part of the Definition of Done.

We now test much earlier in the process and the inclusion of a tester in each team means that there is a constant, direct exchange of information between the developers and the tester. The tester is heavily involved in the planning of each Story and the documentation of acceptance criteria, and is also in constant contact with the Product Owner and other stakeholders.

The continuing automation of regression testing during the Sprints makes it possible to deliver new features faster than before. The entire team has developed a new understanding of the testing process, producing much greater synergy between developers and testers.

Quality assurance is now the joint responsibility of the whole team rather then just the testing team and, as a result, the team is constantly on the lookout for ways to improve its processes.

The agile testers have formed a virtual test team. This Scrum of Testers meets regularly to discuss test automation and testing in general (for example, in Testing Dojos).

Conclusions

The inclusion of management in the changing processes was a critical factor in the success of the switch to Scrum. The switch itself is never really finished and is more of a process of continual improvement. All processes are under continual observation and can always be optimized, leading to the creation of a universal process that blends in perfectly with the existing team and company culture.

8.4   Introducing Scrum at ImmobilienScout24

An interview with Eric Hentschel,
Test Engineer at ImmobilienScout24 in Berlin

ImmobilienScout24 is the largest online real estate agent in the German-speaking countries. According to comScore, the site enjoys more than 7.5 million unique visitors per month. The Berlin-based company has been online for more than 13 years and has more than 500 employees.

About 160 of these are employed in 22 Scrum-based IT development teams. Agile product development has been part of the company's philosophy since 2009 and, as well as Scrum, also includes the use of the hybrid "ScrumBan" development process—a mixture of Scrum and Kanban. Each Scrum Team usually consists of four, five or six developers, the Product Owner, a test engineer, a designer, an architect and an application manager from the production environment.

Reasons for Introducing Scrum

ImmobilienScout24 has grown dynamically over the years. Until 2009, development was based on the traditional V-Model and the staff in a separate QA department were responsible for test analysis, test automation, testing and test management. Test analysis involved a test engineer writing test cases based on the requirements documentation written by product management and also created sequences of test cases as a foundation for test automation. A test automation group then used these sequences to develop automated tests. Communication between product management, development and the QA/testing team was often limited to the context of the test itself, which meant that incomplete or incorrectly interpreted requirements were only discovered at the system testing stage. Like many other companies with software-intensive systems, ImmobilienScout24 had to struggle with the long development cycles, over-large projects, late-stage QA, complex and out-of-date documentation and long release cycles that are often the result of using the V-Model to develop a product. These factors made it difficult to react quickly to customer needs and remedy defects in the online portal.

Nevertheless, the company still managed to build up a solid testing environment. Test cases were managed using the *HP Quality Center* tool and automated using *HP Quick Test Professional*. Up until Scrum was introduced, these systems enabled the company to perform reliable automated regression tests.

A run of all the (manual and automated) regression tests used to take about 12 hours, but could not be repeated at will without manually resetting the test databases. The total time involved in building a release, deploying it in the test environment, evaluating the results of any failed tests and delivering full feedback to the development team usually took about 3-5 days. Reaction times were satisfactory, but the average four-week release cycle for a new version of the portal was still too long. Each four-week cycle included four or five planned release candidates that included corresponding bug fixes and sometimes new features, too. The entire testing process was performed for every release candidate. A four-week release cycle is an impossible dream for many software manufacturers, but Web portals often work on a completely different timescale, making it essential to switch to a faster, more agile development system in order to keep pace with the fast-moving world of high-quality Internet-based commerce.

Making the Switch

The switch to Scrum was begun with a pilot project involving a single team. To begin with, product management, development and QA remained in different physical locations, but communication between them improved significantly thanks to regular standup, effort estimation and Sprint Planning meetings. Because they were still embedded in the existing inflexible test analysis and automation processes, the downstream QA and cumbersome automation processes remained problematic.

A second phase saw additional teams and other departments join the Scrum effort and the physical separation between the individual stakeholders was dissolved. In this context, a separate QA department was no longer sustainable, and each Scrum Team was assigned its own test engineer who was responsible for all test-related tasks (analysis, automation, management and testing itself). Building testing tasks into the team structure significantly accelerated the product development process, but continued use of *HP Quality Center* created a bottleneck in the testing process. Its proprietary scripting language made it impossible for tests to be adapted from within the development team, and changes required the intervention of a dedicated test automation expert, thus lowering the tool's overall level of acceptance. This issue was combated by replacing the HP tool with the Java-based *Selenium 2.0 WebDriver API*. This test framework is under constant development in an active community and enjoys a high level of acceptance among the team's testers and developers. Once the test engineer was able to provide pre-written test cases, the entire development team was able to create and manage automated tests, thus significantly accelerating the test automation process.

The development teams at ImmobilienScout24 are free to choose their own working methods, but most use two-week Scrum cycles. Some teams combine Scrum and Kanban techniques to make an agile system with no predefined Sprint cycles. These teams perform Backlog prioritization and effort estimation the same way as pure Scrum Teams, but don't predefine the number of Stories that is to be included in the next Sprint. Instead, they simply work through the Sprint Backlog from top to bottom, Story by Story.

Obstacles

For the QA staff, the initial phase of the switch to Scrum was an enormous challenge and the newly named team test engineers were faced with a huge expansion of their mandate. The test analysts embedded in each team also had to acquire appropriate development knowledge to enable them to develop automated tests while simultaneously keeping an eye on test analysis. The human element of making such a switch shouldn't be underestimated—at ImmobilienScout24, it took about a year for the teams to get up to speed in the new cross-functional, agile environment.

The replacement of *HP Quality Center* with *WebDriver* and the general advantages of agile methodology significantly improved development speed and quality within the teams.

The dependencies that exist between the individual teams are a function of the complexity of the applications they develop and remain problematic. The nature of the system architecture makes it difficult to draw clear lines between teams and the subsystems they develop. Separate system testing that covers the work of all the development teams is still essential. This type of test will also be necessary in the future but we aim to reduce its complexity as far as possible.

Dissolving the technical dependencies between the various parts of the portal is a huge part of the challenge presented by the switch to agile methodology. Historically, between a third and a fifth of the available resources have been dedicated to IT systems-related projects. In spite of continuing modularization, some larger projects were never completely finished, and the resulting logjams led to the formation of special troubleshooting teams and task forces. The platform's previous monolithic structure has today been largely modularized, although the process is still not completely finished. Database development especially is still prone to bottlenecks, which means that downtime deployment is still occasionally necessary.

Further automation of the testing process also proved difficult, especially with regard to the reproducibility of automated tests of core functionality—tasks that were further complicated by the inconsistent availability of test systems and incomplete test data. Complex database structures, time-consuming data import and database rollbacks also limited reproducibility. There was also no parallel testing capability available.

On the other hand, the temptation to simply automate everything was quite prevalent at the start of the switch to Scrum, especially with regard to development. This led to the creation of large numbers of non-prioritized tests of unclear origin that inevitably led to unstable testing conditions. When analyzing the results of large numbers of tests, it is difficult to distinguish between defects that are the fault of the application and those that are caused by the inherent instability of the system. Additionally, very large numbers of tests are extremely difficult to manage and produce increasingly meaningless results. Attempts to stabilize unstable tests usually fail due to the number and complexity of the potential causes.

Major Changes

Scrum has improved the communication between everyone involved in the development process and has made development generally faster and more efficient. The smaller individual User Stories that are discussed at team level make the requirements clearer and reduce the amount of documentation. The cross-functional nature of Scrum has made all team members much more aware of the work done by the others—a factor that has contributed to a huge increase in product quality.

The downside of this approach is that individual members are oriented more toward their own teams and find it much harder to help out in others. Issues outside of the team are hardly relevant to the test engineers, which leads us directly to the question of just how independent the teams should be. The fact that every team has a relatively free choice of tools and programming languages makes it difficult to alter this team-focused emphasis.

The demands made on management have changed, too. Increasing independence of the teams initially led to a reduction in the amount of coordination effort involved, but the resulting threat of isolation of some teams has led to a renewed increase in coordination effort. Management has to ensure that the development teams continue to work independently while making sure that they respect the Product Owner's priorities and work together to achieve the company's goals. This coordination is achieved using various means, including a weekly AIR Board (Agile Impediment Removal Board) that IT management and the Scrum Masters use to remedy organizational impediments. The Scrum Masters also hold a daily standup meeting to discuss current issues and prevent potential bottlenecks. Product management holds a weekly Epic Board meeting in which the Product Owners discuss the current project status and any planned developments. Development is accompanied from a software and systems point of view by system architects who make sure that the work of the individual teams fits in with the overall concept.

The introduction of Scrum shortened the release cycle by 25%—to three weeks. In the last three years, it has been further shortened to just one week. Release testing now takes place in two phases. Initial regression testing is performed as part of feature development during the Sprint before the integrated release is subjected to a final regression test on a dedicated preview system. This takes the form of exploratory (i.e., manual) tests performed by the existing team of one test manager and five testers, followed by a rerun of the automated tests.

Changes to the Test Procedures

Tests are now an integral part of the Definition of Done, which determines which steps are necessary to complete a Story and roll it out live. The integration of QA in every step of the process reveals defects as early as possible, keeping tests current as well as making them easy to adapt. This approach provides feedback if tests are insufficient or too comprehensive. Because quality is an attribute that developers concentrate on too, it is also easier to consistently implement the agile testing pyramid.

The idea that a single test engineer should be responsible for all functional and non-functional tests has proved impossible to implement. The huge variety of security, load, performance, and automated and exploratory system tests is simply too much for one person to master. The solution lies in getting other dedicated specialists to perform the various additional types of test, such as security tests.

Lessons Learned

The lessons we learned from restructuring our core application and introducing agile development into the teams have led to the construction of a completely new portal. Our market debut in Austria in 2012 gave us the opportunity to build a new product entirely along agile lines. For the Austrian project, we constructed a build environment that enabled Continuous Integration right from the start and everyone involved pursues a quality-oriented development culture. Development is test-driven and weighted according to the agile testing pyramid. Multiple build agents enable parallel testing, giving us fast feedback and new builds with a minimum of commits. The fewer changes and/or commits a build contains, the easier it is to identify the source of any defects that may occur. Targeted modularization makes it possible to alter individual components without affecting other parts of the system. Every test provides its own test data based on predefined conditions and is executable independently of other database states. Data is imported using dedicated internal APIs. Because we don't want to stop regular exploratory testing, not every build results in immediate live deployment, but on average, there is a new live deployment every 24 hours at the latest.

To ensure that the switch to Scrum is a success, you need to pay just as much attention to social factors as you do to technical ones. Our most important lessons were:

- Never forget that people are creatures of habit.
- Dependencies in the system architecture produce dependencies between the individual Scrum Teams that then require active coordination.
- Test-driven development (TDD) and/or Acceptance test-driven development (ATDD) have to be strictly implemented.
- A powerful build environment and test parallelization are essential.
- Automated tests are not a universal remedy. You cannot automate an experienced tester's intuition, and additional exploratory tests are indispensable.

Conclusions

The switch to agile product development involved significant changes in the working methods of many of our employees. The sheer scope of the tasks that our test engineers have to deal with is still a problem and will be addressed by further specialization. Nevertheless, the agile approach is generally felt to be extremely productive. Improved cooperation between team members located physically close to one another has significantly increased testing efficiency. Other major improvements are our improved time to market and a notable reduction in the number of bugs.

8.5   Scrum in a Medical Technology Environment

by Andrea Heck,
Siemens AG Healthcare, Erlangen

Siemens Healthcare (*www.siemens.com/healthcare*) is a worldwide leader in medical imaging and other areas of medical technology. Its *syngo* software is the cornerstone of many of its systems, and forms the foundation for scanning applications and workflow tools that enable hospitals and medical practices to produce high-quality diagnoses and therapies at a reasonable price. *syngo.via* unites all *syngo*-based applications in a sophisticated high-end workplace solution for the appraisal of medical images. Web-based applications also enable medical personnel to view images on the go or at a patient's bedside. This is a highly dynamic market but customers nevertheless expect extremely high-quality results. We also have to adhere to strict national and international laws and guidelines.

The following pages describe the transition to agile project management (with lean elements) made by a development organization that spans seven locations in five countries.

Reasons for Introducing Agile Development and Project Management Techniques

The goals we wanted the transition to achieve were:

- Provide new products and features more quickly to the customer
- Provide better value and higher-quality products that are as closely matched as possible to the needs of the customer
- Motivated and highly efficient development teams
- Reduced costs

The Transition

The transition took place in the three phases that large organizations often use to implement large projects:

1. **Learning and piloting**
   The first agile transition team was formed in 2008 and took a bottom-up approach, learning from other companies and organizations, by studying literature and through visits to conferences and consultants. Management support for the switch was obtained and pilot Scrum Teams were formed. Feedback was analyzed and the results communicated to all staff.
2. **The Big Transition**
   A long preparatory phase of budgeting, external consulting and planning followed. The role of our suppliers changed from that of an extended workbench to a clear partnership. Scrum Teams were trained and implemented and the Product Owner team began its work at an early stage in the process. Many processes, organizational issues and projects were switched in one go in the middle of 2010, and component teams were transformed into Feature Teams. An initial large project with 20 Scrum Teams was started and the teams began the process of continual improvement through self-assessment and coaching.

3. **Continuous Improvement**

   We began to invest more in technical excellence, and the results of Retrospectives began to bear fruit in the form of improvements to processes and tools. We benchmarked ourselves against other similar organizations and lean product development concepts were introduced.

Important principles:

- Every member of the staff contributes to providing value to the
  customer.
- Avoiding waste: Handovers, wait times and overproduction are to be
  prevented, and work-in-progress minimized.
- Suppliers become partners: Suppliers' management is involved in the
  transition process. Joint goals are formulated and each organization
  plans its own implementation. Mutual help takes place where necessary.
- The teams are encouraged to organize themselves, cooperate actively,
  remain critical and constantly question the status quo: Do we work as
  effectively as possible? What can we improve?
- The teams and the Product Owner receive Scrum training. Scrum
  becomes the agile framework in which other agile practices, such as
  XP-based development, are implemented.
- Test phases are pulled forward to take place during development iterations and are run multiple times in the form of regression tests. Test
  automation for existing code is continually improved.
- Continuous learning: Communities of Practice (CoPs) help team
  members to learn beyond the confines of their own teams and to
  improve their performance and technical know-how.

A Significant Challenge: the Change from Component Teams to Feature Teams

In the former, traditional project setup, development was distributed over
multiple locations, and requirement specifications, development and testing took place everywhere. Additionally, the development teams were distributed according to the layers of the application architecture while testers
were distributed according to the test level. The outsourcing strategy prior
to the transition used the extended workbench principle: Individual components were delivered by nearshore and offshore suppliers and each supplier was only responsible for its own components.

Theoretically, the specifications represented the interface. However, because component teams had to separate individual features into many smaller packages, the old system required analysts to prepare each step before integration teams put them together and a whole bunch of interim managers stepped in to solve any integration issues. Even using agile practices, this process produces a mini waterfall effect [Larman/Vodde 09].

We rebuilt the system to form an organization centered around the value chain. This begins with a customer requirement and ends (from the customer's point of view) with a finished product that includes the required feature being installed at the customer site. It is difficult to optimize the value chain in hierarchical organizations that have functional silos, so we organized the teams so that they could each produce a complete value chain. This led to the formation of cross-functional Feature Teams. Each team has its own requirements specialists, software developers, testers and architects. Ideally, developers will come from a variety of component teams and will provide know-how that covers multiple levels within the software architecture.

Unfortunately, this isn't usually sufficient:

Significant know-how is distributed within the teams and shared between them. It can take several months for former specialists to become generalist/specialists.

The major advantage of this setup is that the organization as a whole becomes much more flexible and a single developer can no longer become a bottleneck for multiple features. It also means that most of the program code can now be altered and edited by everyone instead of belonging to a specific team. To help people find their way through the new structure, we named a Component Guardian for each team. This is a person who addresses questions like, "What functionality does component X provide and how is it due to be implemented?" or "Which parts of component X are already covered by automated tests and where do we need to improve coverage?" or "Does the proposed change in the design make sense and does it blend in with the existing functionality?"

A Hierarchical Product Owner Team and the Backlog

To carry out an agile project on this scale, the Product Owner team had to be appropriately scaled. There is now one Chief Product Owner, multiple Product Owners for the individual features and, if necessary, sub-Product

Owners who look after up to three Scrum Teams. There is only one prioritized Product Backlog for the entire product, although this does offer multiple views—for example, only the features on the uppermost layer of the
hierarchy (to define and prioritize the scope and rough content of a version)
or the individual features in a certain area. These can then be broken down
further into the features that are to be dealt with by a specific team and even
further into the features and tasks that belong in a specific Sprint.

Fig. 8–1

*The prioritized Product
Backlog offers various
views of the individual
features. In this illustration, higher priorities are
lower down the list.*

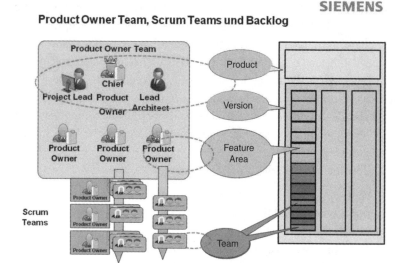

Fulfilling Regulatory Requirements

At the beginning of the project, our process environment was shown to
adhere, for example, to the stipulations of the FDA (Food and Drug
Administration) standards. However, such certification involves significant additional effort, and we ended up asking ourselves whether we could
leave out some non-essential parts of the process to save effort while
achieving the same high-quality results. We also have to keep a constant
lookout for regulations that we can simply ignore because they are already
an integral part of the Scrum and Continuous Integration processes.

Adherence to regulatory requirements is now largely a part of the
doneness criteria that the Product Owner uses to accept features from the
team. For example, our doneness criteria checklist states that in case of a
product risk (i.e., a health risk or potential data loss), appropriate compen-
satory measures have to be built into the feature, too.

Leading FDA consultants nowadays confirm that agile practices are capable of fulfilling the FDA's requirements better than waterfall development techniques [Olivier/Dere 11].

Where Are We Today?

Now, a year later, we have completed our first 20-team Scrum project. Progress within the project was highly transparent from an early stage and we were able to implement timely corrections that enabled us to reach our planned milestones. Most of the teams have plenty of planning and effort estimation experience.

Our Scrum Teams are not yet as efficient as we would like, but are developing in line with our expectations, especially in view of the steep learning curve and enormous amounts of know-how transfer involved. We are still working with some old processes and tools, which we have packed in between our new iterations like slices of sashimi. Introducing agile practices has made our search for wasted effort much more systematic, and we are constantly reviewing processes that appear too complex.

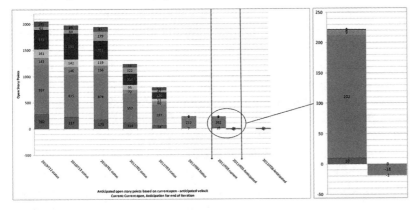

Fig. 8–2

An iteration prior to ending the implementation. At this point, risk levels are low.

Product Owner Team Success

The Product Owner Team regularly invites customers from all over the world to contribute input for planned features. This process often reveals feature priorities that are different from those we were planning to use, enabling us to reprioritize in time. In some cases, the feature and its implementation meet with high levels of customer enthusiasm, while the implementation of other concepts doesn't fit as well with the customer workflow. Such feedback is an important part of the planning process and helps us to alter our basic concepts in time to stay competitive.

The Product Owner Team knows its systems and features very well and performs a comprehensive Sprint Demo of each completed iteration. The Product Owners also help the teams to test workflows and generate feedback by providing informal customer-centric testing input during and after feature development.

We are closer to our goals of delivering the most important features first and orienting our work toward specific customer requirements, but we still need to reduce the length of the complete idea-to-approval cycle.

Development Progress

Our developers now have a much clearer view of the customer's requirements. They discuss the User Stories for new features with the Product Owner and most of them have also been through additional radiology or other specialist training.

Many of the teams have improved their continuous integration skills and they benefit from the availability of a complete set of automated test cases that help them to identify side effects of changes they make. Because the teams no longer work on specific components but instead on the entire code base, developers often add other teams' tests to their own test suites before enhancing a feature. They also feel responsible for adapting test cases that no longer function due to changes in the product code.

Some tests are still automated at too high a level. In other words, we are still testing at the user interface although this is the most time-consuming approach and produces large amounts of correction effort. We were already performing regular code reviews and static code analysis to ensure that we adhere to the prescribed coding guidelines. Code that has not passed these two tests cannot be approved. In addition to testing and code reviews, we have also added pair programming to our QA arsenal. Our developers decide within the team which methods are best for the task(s) at hand. Disciplined pair programming can largely replace code reviews and only safety-related code needs to be checked using additional reviews.

Testing in Scrum Teams

Previously, only unit tests were written and executed by developers, while integration, system and exploratory tests were all performed by specialist testing teams.

Now, the Scrum Teams perform all unit and integration tests for individual components and subsystems. At the start of the project, each Scrum Team had at least one tester who was specially trained to plan and execute tests demanded by regulatory bodies. The appropriate know-how spread accordingly. Cooperation between testers and developers is generally very good and many testers are glad for the opportunity to do some programming. However, in spite of the creative nature of the testing process, developers are not so keen on acquiring new testing skills. Test planning has shown that our current tools are too strongly focused on a central test manager role, thus reducing their acceptance in the teams. We are currently working out how to replace these with more user-friendly tools.

Some developers now write new integration test cases and automate them, and are even busy automating existing test cases. A mid-term advantage of the new process is that new code is better prepared for test automation.

Because a lot of tests and corrections are performed during development, and developers and testers understand the customer requirements better than before, new features have significantly fewer defects that turn up later.

Internal and externally led hands-on coaching within the teams has improved the quality of our test cases and has cut testing time.

The existing test cases had to be newly distributed among the new Feature Teams. Now every test case is assigned to a team that manages it (for example, the conversion from the old *ClearCase* format for use in the new *Team Foundation Server* (TFS) environment). If a team makes a change that breaks a test case, the test has to be repaired by that team before the new code can be released.

Because manual tests are now performed by the teams, test runs initially took longer following the switch to Scrum. Testing time is now slowly being reduced as more tests are automated.

Our Unit Tests (for C# on NUnit) are now completely automated. Our integration tests still include a lot of legacy code with low coverage rates and automation rates of 50-100%, depending on the feature(s) in question.

System Testing

We have a dedicated system testing team that tests code from a customer viewpoint—often in a medical context and on test systems that are equipped with all the necessary RIS and PACS interfaces. Load and stress testing is also performed by this team.

The system testing team develops test cases for new features either parallel to development or in advance of the next iteration. Test cases are automated wherever it makes sense to do so. The non-functional tests have a higher rate of automation than the functional tests.

The system testing team learns about the planned features from the Backlog, from specification details and from the Product Owner. The system testing team also watches the Scrum Teams' Feature Demos and uses its findings to create new customer-centric tests.

The system testing team also performs all official (i.e., documented and signed-off) system tests on specific baselines for specific milestones. These tests take place once repeated automated, exploratory and manual tests have taken place and the system as a whole achieves cumulative coverage of 100%. Electronic reports are sufficient for all other types of tests.

Integration Testing

To guarantee high integration quality, a selection of integration tests is always performed before a code change is added to the baseline. These tests are run on multiple parallel machines and their duration is limited to two hours.

A suite of performance tests runs four times a day for all current code changes. The performance tests use real-world user workflows and have radically reduced the number of performance issues that used to be revealed at later stages of testing.

Fig. 8–3

The trend produced by performance tests run over the course of many iterations.

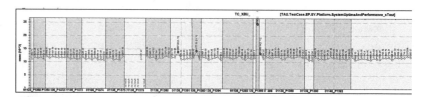

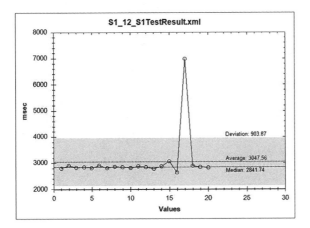

Fig. 8–4

Performance tests are executed several times during each test run and sometimes produce occasional failures.

All automated tests written by all the teams are assembled to form a single large suite that is run on pre-installed test systems (without manual intervention) for every baseline. This approach helps to identify defects that the development teams have missed. Failed tests generate feedback to the Scrum Team that introduced the overlooked dependency. To correct the defect, the team in question will either add the failed test to its own suite or write new, lower-level tests.

What Comes Next?

Continuous improvement is still a major part of future planning:

- Scrum Teams improve their own working methods and environment by means of Retrospectives.
- This takes place in CoPs by means of training, bilateral lectures and know-how transfer.
- Test-driven development and pair programming are practiced in some teams but still not as much as we would like to see. Agile development know-how is constantly being improved through technical coaching, lectures, competitions and demonstrations in the developer CoP.
- Exchange of information with other companies takes place at conferences and through cooperation and mutual benchmarking.
- Strategic projects are initiated to improve processes and tools that have too many interfaces or too much overhead. For example, we have recently replaced *ClearCase* and a proprietary build system with Microsoft's *Team Foundation Server* (TFS).

- Learning from lean principles and methods. A Continual improvement workflow like the one used by Toyota (Kaizen, A3) is to be introduced and we aim to make the systematic solution of problems an integral part of the daily workflow for management and the teams.
- Develop into a learning organization.

Andrea Heck has a university diploma in computer science and has worked in software development for more than 20 years. She is Agile Transition Lead at Siemens Healthcare.

http://www.linkedin.com/in/andreaheck
Blog: *http://andreasagileblog.blogspot.com*

8.6   Testing in Scrum at GE Oil & Gas

An interview with Terry Zuo, Software Manager
at the Software Development Center (SSDC),
Measurement & Control, GE Oil & Gas in Shanghai, China.

GE Oil & Gas is a world leader in advanced technologies and services with 37,000 employees in more than 100 countries supporting customers across the industry—from Oil & Gas extraction to transportation to end use. GE Measurement & Control (M&C), one of the key members in GE Oil & Gas, improves the health and productivity of power plants, refineries, and other critical industry systems through advanced sensing, testing, control, and monitoring technologies and is a leading innovator in advanced, sensor-based measurement, nondestructive testing, inspection and condition monitoring. and flow and process control solutions (e.g. business platforms and supporting tools). GE M&C serves 2 million end users each month around the globe.

Reasons for Switching to Agile

In GE, we used the model of product lines, regions, and functions (dot line report the global business leader, direct to the function leaders), which means that all the organizations have matrix reports. This model is designed for the operative business, but the engineering project execution includes the following cons:

- Complex decision-making structure can make Product Owner role challenging
- Regional, product, and global function influences

To overcome these shortcomings and to accelerate delivery, GE Oil & Gas in 2008 started the adoption of Scrum and agile practices. This transition has been steadily growing over the past five years, and now in 2013 it encompasses more than 150 teams in the United States, Europe, and Asia-Pacific.

Transition at GE

So, how have we achieved these goals of quick decision and fast execution effectively and at the same time involved our current QMS system to respond to the high demand of being agile? The engineering team worked out and implemented of the following activities:

- Reinvigorating GE's Lean Six Sigma™/agile culture
  - Ramping up team of Black Belts and Master Black Belts to focus on key issues
  - Working together with various teams, we have identified where we can make the biggest impact through projects and initiatives.
- Increasing Lean Six Sigma/agile knowledge and DNA
  - Offering online Lean Six Sigma and agile/Scrum courses in the GE online learning platform.
  - Conducting Green Belt training classes for individuals leading key projects.
  - Identifying individuals to participate as team members on action workouts and key projects.
- Connecting QMS, Lean Six Sigma, and Agile
  - We used QMS and Lean development previously. There are still a few different points, but even Agile does have connection with Lean. We borrowed a lot of good points from Lean and did a deep analysis in terms of how we can identify the lean approach and highlight the agile practice.

Fig. 8–5

Agile Methods
as a Lean approach
(©2014 GE, used by
permission of GE)

Agile methods can be interpreted as a *Lean approach to IT project*
management and execution.

Lean Approach	Agile Practice
Kaizen Continuous improvement	Iteration Planning Sessions Process & Project Reflections
Kanban Visual management systems	Product backlogs Iteration backlogs Burndown charts Project and quality sliders Automated test dashboards
Setup reduction Adaptability to rapid change	Automated builds Continuous integration Test-driven development Automated testing
Takt time Delivery based on customer demand	Iterative development cycles Incremental development
Work cells Co-located resources for a given task	Cross-functional teams Collaborative team environments Generalizing specialist roles Pair Programming

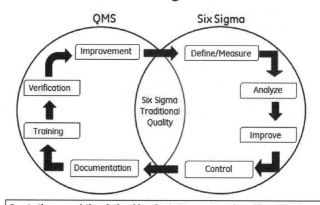

QMS and Lean Six Sigma

Due to the synergistic relationship, the QMS cannot survive without Six Sigma and Six Sigma needs the QMS to monitor and provide feedback on projects.

The Transition at the Shanghai SSDC Team

The Shanghai SSDC team started transition in late 2008 with two pilots. One of those was the implementation of our HMI platform. Through this pilot, we demonstrated a 20 percent increase in productivity primarily by avoiding the implementation of features of limited value that would have been implemented using our classic waterfall method. We also were able to adjust our design for changing business requirements and for our evolving understanding of what capabilities were of the greatest value. On top of all that, we improved user satisfaction and the satisfaction of employees engaged in the project.

So, that got us excited about the full potential of agile, and we proceeded to drive a transformation to agile for all projects where it makes sense. Finally, the HR & Top management team helped review the current resource and reorganized with the typical Scrum project team structure:

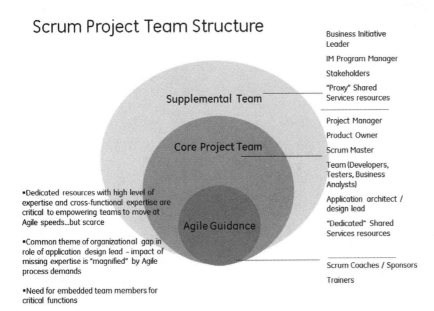

Fig. 8–6
Scrum Project Team Structure (©2014 GE, used by permission of GE)

During the transition from waterfall to agile/Scrum, we identified the roles of project manager and Product Owner as a pair. To move forward smoothly, the role of project manager was kept and adapted to Scrum practice. The team updated the ideas according to its daily work and practice. Here are the key ideas:

- Product Owner duties shared between business Product Owner and project manager.
- The Scrum Master is the predominant role in pilot projects.
- Importance of embedded QA resources, experienced design resources, and Business Analysis (BA) ressources.
- Emphasized Flex model for shared services resources.

	2009	2011	2012	2013
Source control and branching	VSS	TFS		TFS
TDD/BDD	**TDD** is a highly recommended practice. Unit Tests are must have for every user story.	New code is covered by unit tests. The situation is worse on C# side, we just started TDD adoption for UI. Early attempts to use BDD.		Clear focus on BDD.
Automated Functional Tests	Some **Selenium/TestComplete** tests.	Automated functional tests are based on TC/Selenium. We've created a framework in C# to simplify tests development.	**Functional tests** run in parallel. Test coverage is much better.	
Continuous Integration	Very basic.	Very basic.	We use Cruise Control and have quite many different setups. **Smoke builds, release builds**, etc. Functional tests run in parallel and it takes 1 hour to run them all.	The goal is to have a Continuous Delivery process eventually.
Test Coverage	don't measure		We have 10% unit tests coverage and 30% functional tests coverage	We have 20% unit tests coverage and 50% functional tests coverage

Fig. 8–7
Transition at SSDC

With company/team growth, we've replaced a single large team with several mini-teams. A mini-team is fully responsible for Epic design and implementation and usually consists of the Product Owner, designer, one to three developers, one or two testers, and the writer. A mini-team makes all technical decisions, brainstorms ideas, and provides solutions. It is autonomous and focused and enables us to operate more effectively and respond more quickly. Currently we have six mini-teams at SDDC Shanghai. Reviewing the process changes for the last five years, the following observations were made:

- **Points—No Estimates:** This shift became possible with Kanban adoption. Clearly, you should estimate work in iterative development. Now we have only horizon-level estimates like "days," "weeks," "month," "months." Sometimes the Product Owner misses the estimates, but with the new road map plans, horizon-level estimates got surprisingly accurate.

- **Time tracking—No time tracking:** We tracked the spent time from day 1. Time tracking was deep inside us, and even salary was based on the hours spent. It was quite a difficult decision to break this rule, but everything went surprisingly smooth. Actually, there are almost no reasons to track time if you don't estimate work. Some people complained initially, but in two to three months, everybody was happy with the decision. Finally, we tracked the PBI status.

- **Release Planning—None—Road maps:** These transitions might seem a bit strange. Initially we did strict release planning, but with Kanban adoption, we quit this practice. It appeared to us that it wasn't a very good idea. The problem was that we lost the focus. A release with a clear focus is a very good thing; it helps define what should be done and what shouldn't. Without the focus, you do many small and large things that don't feature a common goal. That blurs development effort and you release just a set of features. So we decided to use road maps instead. There can be three to four large Epics in development. Each Epic has a clear goal and takes 3 to 12 months to complete. The road map just shows all Epics in progress and some future Epics.
- **User stories split:** The funny thing is that we still don't get it. In our case, the user stories are always high-level features combined with domain standards, and it is not easy to split them. However, we strictly followed the INVEST model these years, which really helps us to improve user stories.
- **Daily meeting:** This practice survived five years without modifications. We tried to keep it short and concrete. We can easily run a meeting with 15 people in 15 minutes.
- **Meetings:** The trend is to have fewer general meetings and more focused ones. The only periodic meeting we have right now is a daily meeting; the rest are on demand. In Scrum, you have many formal meetings, which may be good if you've just started agile adoption. With time, they tend to deplete. Just-in-time meetings are great: fewer people, better focus, and better results.

Major Changes

In the past years, all engineering teams moved from waterfall to Scrum, and the following actions occurred in our unit, which really improved the daily work efficiency and reduced the cost as well. Not only did the operations rhythm changed, the way we work impacted the overall project performance:

- Job roles and hiring requirements adjusted
- Overall organizational structure and workspace realigned

- Traction in modern practices and teams' operating rhythm in place and working well:
  - Daily / Sprint / Release / Release Train
  - 100 percent Continuous Integration
- Enthusiastic cultural shift in 2012

Results and Benefits

- 96 out of ~267 system releases followed the agile methodology.
- 91 percent of our agile releases hit our release date commitment.
- After each release, we measure overall client satisfaction with the results and execution. Satisfaction is measured on a scale of 1 to 10. Average score for the releases was 8.8, a .4 increase over waterfall.
- The other big benefit that we realized was dramatically reduced time to delivering products: average time from start to first release or time between releases in a project was 4 months. For our classic waterfall process, it was one year!

Some of the accelerated cycle time we saw was due to the types of projects, however, but Agile contributed to at least a 2x acceleration. Nothing boosts client confidence and excitement more than when they get a solution of value in their hands dramatically faster. Employees and our contracts get fired up too!

Lessons Learned

- Obstacles
  - Not willing to change.
  - Clear roles and responsibilities with agile/Scrum model.
  - Setting up a general one-fits-all test automation framework is a journey; it needs continuous efforts.
  - Continuous Integration needs effort.
- Overall key factors for success
  - Capturing and transferring agile methodology knowledge provides consistent execution, responsibility, accountability.
  - Ensuring that products and services are delivered to the satisfaction of our customers increases reputation, growth, innovation, and customer loyalty.

- Identifying key metrics for future process improvements to eliminate waste, perform only value-added activities, permanently solve issues (quality, performance, teaming, etc.), and drive solutions to improve products and services.
- Staffing-related lessons learned
  - Allocate a dedicated full-time transformation leader!
  - No coaches/experts, no agile. So invest in coaching capacity, hire full-time employee coaches sooner, and distribute coaches globally.
  - Require agile expertise in recruiting/job requirements.
  - Hire Scrum Master roles.
  - Modify formal project management methodology.
  - Adopt points-based contracting. The performance of staff depends on a system covered with growth values and measured points, which will impact the staff's contract and promotion plan.
  - Federate specialized expertise/center of excellence

Conclusions and What's Next

The agile team at SSDC has more than doubled in size and continues to grow. Although we have over 150 agile teams at M&C, we still have a long way to go. Some teams are very agile; others do mini-waterfalls and call it agile. Change is difficult, and to change a company as large as GE sometimes feels like trying to steer a giant ship with a small paddle. We have learned that patience is important, as is remembering that even the smallest of incremental improvements can have a massive payoff when you do them on a large scale. As we become more mature with our agile practices, we will significantly increase our velocity:

- More test automation is critical to accelerating build and test cycles while improving the quality of our output.
- Test-driven development:
  - Forces robust understanding of the purpose of components
  - Ensures that all modules have robust automated testing
  - Only just starting to play with this in IT
- Continuous Integration
  - Ensures that we can always of an integrated build of a system ready for testing and release

- Forces incremental fixing of conflicts and issues across independent modules that eliminates the fixing of overwhelming build issues
- Requires automated builds that reduces overall build/test cycle time

The agile team and strategy continues to evolve. Our only constant is change.

Appendix

A   Glossary

Term	Definition	Source
acceptance criteria	The exit criteria that a component or system must satisfy in order to be accepted by a user, customer, or other authorized entity	[URL: ISTQB Glossary]
acceptance testing	Formal testing with respect to user needs, requirements, and business processes conducted to determine whether or not a system satisfies the acceptance criteria and to enable the user, customers or other authorized entity to determine whether or not to accept the system	[URL: ISTQB Glossary]
agile software development	A group of software development methods based on iterative and incremental development, where requirements and solutions evolve through collaboration between self-organizing, cross-functional teams. It promotes adaptive planning, evolutionary development and delivery, a timeboxed iterative approach, and encourages rapid and flexible response to change. It is a conceptual framework that promotes foreseen tight interactions throughout the development cycle.	*http://en.wikipedia.org/wiki/ Agile_software_development*
agile testing	Testing practice for a project using agile software development methodologies, incorporating techniques and methods, such as Extreme Programming (XP), treating development as the customer of testing and emphasizing the Test First design paradigm	after *[URL: ISTQB Glossary]*
build	A compiled version of software, or the process of producing it	*http://en.wikipedia.org/wiki/ Build*
compliance	The state or fact of according with or meeting rules or standards	*http:// www.oxforddictionaries.com*
component	1. A software item of minimal complexity that can be tested in isolation 2. A software item that conforms to the implementation guideline of a certain software component model (EJB, CORBA, .NET etc.)	after [Spillner/Linz 2014]

Term	Definition	Source
data-driven test	A scripting technique that stores test input and expected results in a table or spreadsheet, so that a single control script can execute all of the tests in the table	[URL: ISTQB Glossary]
depended-on component (DOC)	An individual class or a large-grained component on which the system under test (SUT) depends	[Meszaros 07]
deployment	All activities that make a software system available for use, especially its installation and activation within the execution environment	after *http://en.wikipedia.org/wiki/Software_deployment*
domain specific language (DSL)	A computer programming language of limited expressiveness, focused on a particular domain	[Fowler/Parsons 10]
dummy	A placeholder object that is passed to the SUT as an argument (or an attribute of an argument) because it is syntactically required, but never actually used	after [Meszaros 07]
fake	An object that is neither directly controlled nor observed by the test and that replaces the functionality of the real DOC with an alternative (simplified) implementation	after [Meszaros 07]
functional test (box test)	1. Verification of functional requirements 2. Testing based on an analysis of the specification of the functionality of a component or system	after [Spillner/Linz 14]
integration	The process of combining components into larger assemblies	[Spillner/Linz 14]
integration test	Testing performed to expose defects in the interfaces and in the interactions between integrated components or systems	[Spillner/Linz 14]
mock	An "intelligent" stub that returns different results to the SUT depending on the parameters it is called with (by the SUT). Acts as an observation point for the indirect output of the SUT.	after [Meszaros 07]
non-functional test	Testing the attributes of a component or system that do not relate to functionality—e.g., reliability, efficiency, usability, maintainability and portability	[Spillner/Linz 14]
performance test (load test)	Tests that determine the changes of performance of a software product with increasing load	after [Spillner/Linz 14]
quality management	Coordinated measures to manage an organization with respect to quality	[ISO 9000]
quality assurance	All measures quality management measures that are focused on generating confidence that a product's quality requirements will be fulfilled	after [Spillner/Linz 14]

Term	Definition	Source
quality assurance, analytical	Diagnostic-based measures—for example, testing to measure or evaluate the quality of a product	[Spillner/Linz 14]
quality assurance, preventive	Use of methods, tools and procedures that contribute to enhancing the design quality of the product. As a result of their application, development errors are avoided or the probability of their occurrence reduced, resulting in a product with only the desired characteristics and few defects.	after [Spillner/Linz 14]
Sprint Retrospective	The Sprint Retrospective is an opportunity for the Scrum Team to inspect itself and create a plan for improvements to be enacted during the next Sprint. The Sprint Retrospective occurs after the Sprint Review and prior to the next Sprint Planning.	[URL: Scrum Guide]
Keyword-driven testing	A scripting technique that uses data files to contain not only test data and expected results, but also keywords related to the application being tested. The keywords are interpreted by special supporting scripts that are called by the control script for the test.	[URL: ISTQB Glossary]
Scrum	A framework within which people can address complex adaptive problems while productively and creatively delivering products of the highest possible value. The Scrum framework consists of Scrum Teams and their associated roles, events, artifacts and rules.	after [URL: Scrum Guide]
Simulator	A device, computer program or system used during testing, which behaves or operates like a given system when provided with a set of controlled inputs	[URL: ISTQB Glossary]
Sprint	A time-box of one month or less during which a "Done", useable and potentially releasable product increment is created. Sprints consist of Sprint Planning, Daily Scrums, the development work itself, the Sprint Review and the Sprint Retrospective.	after [URL: Scrum Guide]
spy	A stub with the additional capability of silently recording all calls made to its methods. The logged data can be used to verify the SUT's indirect output.	after [Meszaros 07]
stub	An object that replaces a DOC with an object that has an identical interface so that the test can control the indirect inputs of the SUT	after [Meszaros 07]
system test	A test of an integrated system to verify that it meets the specified requirements	after [Spillner/Linz 14]
testing pyramid	A metaphor for the set of all planned or existing test cases and their distribution between the unit, integration and system testing levels	

Term	Definition	Source
unit test (component test)	Test of a single (isolated) software component	
validation	Confirmation by examination and through provision of objective evidence that the requirements for a specific intended use or application have been fulfilled	[ISO 9000]
verification	Confirmation by examination and through the provision of objective evidence that specified requirements have been fulfilled	[ISO 9000]

B References

B.1 Literature

[Aho et al. 06]

Alfred Aho, Monica Lam, Ravi Sethi, Jeffrey Ullman
Compilers: Principles, Techniques, and Tools
Addison Wesley, 2nd edition, 2006

[Anderson 10]

David J. Anderson
Kanban: Successful Evolutionary Change for Your Technology Business
Blue Hole Press, 2010

[Bashir/Goel 99]

Imran Bashir, Amrit Goel
Testing Object-Oriented Software: Life Cycle Solutions
Springer, New York, 1999 (reprint 2012)

[Beck/Andres 04]

Kent Beck, Cynthia Andres
Extreme Programming Explained: Embrace Change (2nd edition)
Addison-Wesley Longman, Amsterdam, 2004.

[Beedle et al. 99]

Mike Beedle, Martine Devas, Yonat Sharon, Ken Schwaber, Jeff Sutherland
Scrum: An Extension Pattern Language for Hyperproductive Software
Development
Addison-Wesley Longman, Amsterdam, 1999

[Bergmann/Priebsch 11]

Sebastian Bergmann, Stefan Priebsch
Real-World Solutions for Developing High-Quality PHP Frameworks and
Applications Wrox, 2011

[Crispin/Gregory 08]

Lisa Crispin, Janet Gregory
Agile Testing: A Practical Guide for Testers and Agile Teams
Addison-Wesley Longman, Amsterdam, 2008.

[Duvall et al. 07]

Paul M. Duvall, Steve Matyas, Andrew Glover
Continuous Integration: Improving Software Quality and Reducing Risk
Addison-Wesley Signature Series, 2007.

[Fowler/Parsons 10]

Martin Fowler, Rebecca Parsons
Domain-Specific Languages
Addison-Wesley Signature Series, 2010.

[Ghosh 11]

Debasish Ghosh
DSLs in Action
Manning, 2011

[Gutmans et al. 04]

Andy Gutmans, Stig Bakken, Derick Rethans
PHP 5 Power Programming
Prentice Hall, 2005

[Larman/Vodde 09]

Craig Larman, Bas Vodde
Scaling Lean and Agile Development
Addison-Wesley Longman, Amsterdam, 2009.

[Link 03]

Johannes Link
Unit Testing in Java: How Tests Drive the Code
Morgan Kaufmann, 2003

[Malik 09]

Fredmund Malik
Managing Performing Living: Effective Management for a New Era
Campus Verlag, 2009

[Martin 08]

Robert C. Martin
Clean Code: A Handbook of Agile Software Craftsmanship
Prentice Hall, 2008.

[Meszaros 07]

Gerard Meszaros
xUnit Test Patterns: Refactoring Test Code
Addison-Wesley Signature Series, 2007.

[Olivier/Dere 11]

Dan Olivier, Jeff Dere
Agile Software Development Streamlines FDA-Regulated Applications
In Medical Electronics Design, April 2011.

[Pichler 10]
Roman Pichler
Agile Product Management with Scrum: Creating Products that Customers Love
Addison-Wesley Signature Series, 2010.

[Pichler/Roock 11]
Roman Pichler, Stefan Roock
Agile Entwicklungspraktiken mit Scrum, dpunkt.verlag, Heidelberg, 2011

[Rahien 10]
Ayende Rahien
DSLs in Boo: Domain-Specific Languages in .NET
Manning, 2010

[Schwaber/Beedle 02]
Ken Schwaber, Mike Beedle
Agile Software Development with Scrum
Pearson Prentice Hall, 2002

[Schlossnagle 04]
George Schlossnagle,
Advanced PHP Programming,
Sams Publishing, 2004

[Spillner/Linz 14]
Andreas Spillner, Tilo Linz, Hans Schaefer
Software Testing Foundations, 4th Edition
Rocky Nook, 2014

[Vigenschow 10]
Uwe Vigenschow, Testen von Software und Embedded Systems, Professionelles
Vorgehen mit modellbasierten und objektorientierten Ansätzen, dpunkt.verlag,
Heidelberg, 2010

[Winter et al. 12]
Mario Winter, Mohsen Ekssir-Monfared, Harry Sneed, Lars Borner, Richard
Seidl: Der Integrationstest. Hanser Verlag, München, 2012

B.2   Websites[1]

[URL: Agile Manifesto]
Manifesto for Agile Software Development, *http://agilemanifesto.org*

[URL: Agile Testing]
http://en.wikipedia.org/wiki/Agile_testing

[URL: BDT]
http://en.wikipedia.org/wiki/Behavior-driven_development

---

1.   URLs valid as per February 2014

[URL: FMC]

Fundamental Modeling Concepts,
http://www.fmc-modeling.org

[URL: iAkad]

Testing in SCRUM, Training course of imbus academy,
http://www.imbus.de/akademie

[URL: iCAT]

Certified Agile Tester, Training scheme and learning objectives, International
Software Quality Institute GmbH
http://www.agile-tester.org/syllabus.html

[URL: ISTQB Glossary]

ISTQB® Glossary of Testing Terms, Version 2.2
http://www.istqb.org/downloads.html

[URL: ISTQB]

International Software Testing Qualifications Board, *http://www.istqb.org*
Austrian Testing Board, *http://www.austriantestingboard.org*
German Testing Board, *http://www.german-testing-board.org*
Swiss Testing Board, *http://www.swiss-testing-board.ch*

[URL: Lean]

Lean (project) management
http://en.wikipedia.org/wiki/Lean_project_management

Lean manufacturing
http://en.wikipedia.org/wiki/Lean_manufacturing

[URL: OMG]

OMG Specifications, *http://www.omg.org/spec/index.htm*

[URL: PDCA]

http://en.wikipedia.org/wiki/PDCA

[URL: PHP]

Homepage of the PHP project: manuals, downloads, news, *http://www.php.net*

[URL: PHPUnit]

PHPUnit Manual,
http://www.phpunit.de/manual/current/en/automating-tests.html

[URL: RUP]

http://en.wikipedia.org/wiki/IBM_Rational_Unified_Process

[URL: Scrum Guide]

The Scrum Guide, Developed and sustained by Ken Schwaber
and Jeff Sutherland, *http://www.scrum.org*

[URL: SUnit]

http://en.wikipedia.org/wiki/SUnit

[URL: SWT-knowledge]

book web page, *http://www.softwaretest-knowledge.net*

[URL: Testtoolreview]

information platform on the international market of software testing tools, classified by application areas, *https://www.testtoolreview.com*

[URL: W3C]

http://www.w3.org/standards

[URL: W3C validator]

http://validator.w3.org

B.3   Standards

[DO 178 B]

DO-178B, Software Considerations in Airborne Systems and Equipment Certification, Issued 12-1-92, Prepared by RTCA SC-167, Supersedes DO-178A, Errata Issued 3-26-99, *www.rtca.org*

[EN 50128]

EN 50128:2011, Railway applications – Communication, -signalling and processing systems – Software for railway control and protection systems

[IEC 62304]

IEC 62304:2006, Medical device software – software life cycle processes.

[FDA OTS]

Guidance for Industry, FDA Reviewers and Compliance on -
Off-The-Shelf Software Use in Medical Devices, September 9, 1999, *http://www.fda.gov/MedicalDevices*

[FDA Validation]

General Principles of Software Validation; Final Guidance for Industry and FDA Staff, January 11, 2002, *http://www.fda.gov/MedicalDevices*

[IEC 61508-3]

IEC 61508-3:2010: Functional safety of electrical/electronic/programmable electronic safety-related systems – Part 3: Software requirements

[IEEE 610]

IEEE Std 610.12-1990, IEEE Standard Glossary of Software – Engineering Terminology

[IEEE 730]

IEEE Std 730-2002, IEEE Standard for Software Quality – Assurance Plans

[IEEE 829]

IEEE Std 829-2008, IEEE Standard for Software and System Test Documentation

[IEEE 1044]

IEEE Std 1044-1993, IEEE Standard Classification for Software Anomalies.

[ISO 9000]

EN ISO 9000:2005, Quality management systems – Fundamentals and vocabulary

[ISO 9001]

EN ISO 9001:2008, Quality management systems – Requirements

[ISO 9126]

ISO/IEC 9126-1:2001 Software engineering – Product quality – Part 1: Quality model, Revised by in ISO/IEC 25010:2011

ISO/IEC TR 9126-2:2003 Software engineering – Product quality – Part 2: External metrics

ISO/IEC TR 9126-3:2003 Software engineering – Product quality – Part 3: Internal metrics

ISO/IEC TR 9126-4:2004, Software engineering – Product quality – Part 4: Quality in use metrics

[ISO 9241]

ISO 9241-x, Ergonomics of human-system interaction, -Normenreihe

[ISO 12207]

ISO/IEC 12207:2008-02, Systems and software engineering – Software life cycle processes

[ISO 25000]

ISO/IEC 250xy, Software Engineering – Software product – Quality Requirements and Evaluation (SquaRE), Normenreihe

[ISO 25010]

ISO/IEC 25010:2011, Systems and software engineering – Systems and software Quality Requirements and Evaluation (SQuaRE) – System and software quality models

[ISO 26262]

ISO 26262-6:2011-11, Road vehicles – Functional safety, Part 6: Product development at the software level

[ISO 29119]

ISO/IEC/IEEE 29119, Software and systems engineering — Software testing, First edition, 2013-09-01

Part 1: Concepts and definitions, Part 2: Test processes, Part 3: Test documentation

Index